GREAT
OPERA HOUSES
MASTERPIECES OF ARCHITECTURE

GREAT OPERA HOUSES

MASTERPIECES OF ARCHITECTURE

ANDRAS KALDOR

ANTIQUE COLLECTORS' CLUB

First published 1996 as *Opera Houses of Europe*
Re-issued 2002, with additional material, as *Great Opera Houses – Masterpieces of Architecture*
© Antique Collectors' Club and Andras Kaldor
Illustrations © 1996 and 2002 Andras Kaldor
World copyright reserved

ISBN 1 85149 363 8

British Library Cataloguing-in-Publication Data
A catalogue record for this book is available from the British Library

Edited extracts on pages 38 and 39 from 'Designing the Rake's Progress', by Martin Friedman and
David Hockney in *Hockney Paints the Stage,* exhibition catalogue, Walker Art Center, Minneapolis, MN,
published by Abbeville Press, 1983, NY

Extract on pages 46 and 47 from Georg Solti's autobiography, *Solti,*
1997, Chatto & Windus (UK), Alfred A. Knopf (US)

Extract on pages 74 and 75 from *Galina: A Russian Story*, English translation
copyright © 1984 by Galina Vishnevskaya and Harcourt Brace & Company, reprinted by
permission of the publisher

Detail on page 1 shows a decorative panel at the Národní Divadlo
The frontispiece shows the Palais Garnier, Paris, at night
The title page shows the Sydney Opera House
Detail on page 6 shows an architectural detail from the Markgräfliches Opernhaus, Bayreuth
Detail on page 126 shows a fountain at the Staatsoper, Vienna
Detail on page 128 shows a decorative panel at the Théâtre Royal de la Monnaie, Brussels

Printed in Italy
Published by the Antique Collectors' Club Limited, Woodbridge, Suffolk IP12 4SD

CONTENTS

To Sally
companion on all my travels

PREFACE

As the enjoyment and popularity of opera is growing, perhaps it is opportune to draw attention to the splendid houses built for the purpose of performing grand opera. The 18th and 19th centuries, when most of them were built, saw an optimistic mini-Renaissance in between wars and revolutions. No other period has produced so many composers of grand opera, or the enthusiasm of the citizens to build and support these great edifices.

The histories of the buildings are no less dramatic than the operas performed within. They were often at the centre of dissent and political upheaval. Fires, earthquakes, floods and war at one time or another have destroyed most of them. Many of them have been rebuilt, often more splendidly than before.

One of the few advantages of growing up in post-war Budapest was that an evening at the opera was a frequent and affordable event – even compulsory when Grandfather was a spear carrier in *Aïda* or a peasant in *Boris Godunov*. Grandfather's enthusiasm stayed with me ever since. Appreciation of the architecture of opera houses took a little longer.

After some twenty years in architectural practice and with scant chance of working on such elaborate buildings, the decision to record some of these splendid houses was an easy one. Sally, my wife, and I set off on three separate journeys to visit the opera houses of Europe and paint the pictures you are about to see and, I hope, enjoy.

On our way we soon developed a simple system as we came to each opera house. Sally went off to research its history, and I made colour sketches and took photographs. As most of the houses are in the busy centre of town, setting up an easel is quite impossible.

Back in my studio the information was assembled, the pen and ink drawing done and then the painting – the most exciting part – using the sketches for the true colours.

This process of reconstructing the buildings on paper from the collected details allowed an insight into the minds of those architects whose task it was to create these symbols of cultural eminence. If the paintings allow the reader the same insight the purpose of the book is achieved.

The task of compiling this book was made more enjoyable by the assistance and advice of friends old and new. My grateful thanks to Graeme Kay for his invaluable help and contributions in all matters operatic; to Stephenson B. Andrews for writing so many of the 'historics' of opera houses; to all the contributors who have so generously given their help and told their stories for this book; and to Ashutosh Khandekar, Editor-in-Chief of *Opera Now* for his advice.   Andras Kaldor, Dartmouth, September 1996

This revised edition of *Opera Houses of Europe* has been expanded to include opera houses from further afield Travelling to exhibitions in London, Budapest and New York with the original paintings from the first book, gave me the chance to record more opera houses, and these have now been added. Although there are still some one hundred and thirty more to go before I've visited and painted all the opera houses in the world, it is an ambition I aim to fulfil.   Andras Kaldor, Dartmouth, September 2001

INTRODUCTION

Opera and architecture have always been inextricably linked in my imagination. The first opera I attended was one I was in: Benjamin Britten's *Noye's Fludde,* based on the Biblical story of Noah's ark, in which I had a solo part. So successful was the production in my Scottish grammar school (functional, modern school hall with shallow proscenium stage, no flying facilities) that we were invited to present it in the vast space of Dunfermline Abbey (no facilities of any kind). We set up our rostra, ark and giant rainbow in the magnificent Norman nave – and I was roundly rebuked by the director for gazing, somewhat in awe, around the darkened, echoing interior whenever I wasn't singing. Even at the age of twelve, I was beginning to be aware of the symbiotic relationship between performing and the space in which the performance takes place.

Another indispensable part of my upbringing in central Scotland was the annual visit to the pantomime: I am sure that my passion for theatres was born in the opulent Rococo-style surroundings of the 1906 King's Theatre in Edinburgh, or its Glasgow counterpart, Frank Matcham's 1904 theatre, also the King's, where no Christmas was complete without Stanley Baxter. And I also became dimly aware that traditional theatres imply certain . . . social distinctions. On one occasion Baxter was engaged in a dialogue with the audience – as the theatre-goers called out their answers to his questions, he suddenly pointed an accusing finger at the boxes: 'I'm not talking to you posh folk in the ash-trays, I'm talking to my friends doon here.' Those comfortable Scottish burghers who had paid more to sit enveloped in an extra measure of 'Rococo' privacy took the jibe in good part.

It was only later, when I began to study opera and theatres more seriously, that I was able to understand the historical significance of Baxter's remark. When opera theatres began to be purpose-built – good examples would be the Palais Garnier in Paris and the Royal Opera House, Covent Garden – the opulence of the interiors, with their grand staircases, mirrors and chandeliers, was intended to reflect the social status and aspirations of their wealthy and aristocratic patrons. As such, so went the orthodoxy, the denizens of the cheap seats in the gods would be as discomfited by the presence of such finery, as the grandees would be to turn a corner in the Crush Bar and be confronted by a group of horny-handed sons of toil; and so, the latter had their own entrance, usually down an alley and involving a precipitous climb up an undecorated and faintly malodorous staircase. This architectural habit persisted into the 20th century – the London Coliseum (Matcham 1904) and Sadler's Wells Theatre (1931, demolished 1996) are good examples.

But while sparing a thought for the people perched in the Upper Slips (didn't we all start our opera-going up there?), the point about front-of-house spaces is that – cramped or expansive – they are mere preparation for the grand entrance into the auditorium itself.

One of the best of these experiences is to step up from the bar into the orchestra stalls at Covent Garden: your eyes are drawn first to the bright blue-gold ceiling; then, as you emerge from the depths, your gaze descends to the gold barley-sugar of the proscenium arch, reflecting the twinkling lights of the auditorium's candle-sconces, and finally come to rest on the deep burgundy velvet of the house tabs and their gold royal crest.

Each opera house offers its own individual thrill. At the Festspielhaus in Bayreuth it's the cowl over the orchestra pit which hides the orchestra and conductor from view, and sets up the 'mystic gulf' between artists and audience – and what sound! At the Palais Garnier and the State Opera House in Budapest, it's the sumptuous décor. By contrast, at the Royal Court Theatre in Drottningholm, it's the dim light and the smell of sheer *antiquity* in the tiny wooden auditorium.

While the interiors of opera houses make their impact on opera-goers and the curious visitor, the buildings themselves help to define the cities they inhabit: a town without a theatre is not much of a town.

Wagner's Festspielhaus, sitting atop its 'green hill', dominates the town of Bayreuth which before 1876 had to make do only with one of the most spectacular of all the Baroque theatres, the Markgräfliches Opernhaus of 1748. The power and status of the Národní Divadlo in Prague is reflected fully in the waters of the River Vltava which flow past, just as Operan, the Royal Opera in Stockholm, looks across the river to the magnificent royal palace. Nor is anyone going to miss the Palais Garnier or the Semperoper in Dresden, which dominate their respective urban surroundings.

Wherever you go in search of opera and its theatres, Andras Kaldor will have been there before you. No one who loves the complementary arts of music and architecture could fail to admire his work. To the painter's art he brings the architect's eye for detail, but not slavishly so: his theatres exude personality, and personality is more than the sum of individual parts.

With theatres, you never know what's round the corner – destruction or development? The razing of the Gran Teatre del Liceu in Barcelona (1994) and La Fenice in Venice (1996) reminds us that the technological advances of the late 20th century allow for no complacency in respect of the theatre heritage, and provide an unwelcome reminder, documented in these pages, of all those catastrophic theatre fires of the 18th and 19th centuries.

I believe that *Great Opera Houses* will provide pleasure and satisfaction for everyone who has the book in their library, and – now that the travel barriers all across the Continent are down – may spur us on to 'collect' those theatres we have not yet visited. I commend it to you.   Graeme Kay, Online Producer and Presenter BBC Radio 3

THE CONTRIBUTORS

Stephenson B. Andrews is an architectural historian and private curator in Washington, New York and London, dealing with projects for collectors, commercial galleries and institutions in Europe and the United States.

Miklós Borsa has been Technical Director at the Budapest Opera House – Magyar Állami Operaház – for the past thirty-two years and is author of *The Unknown Opera House.*

Julio Bravo writes for the cultural section of the Madrid daily newspaper *ABC.*

Brendan Carroll is a writer, critic and opera lover.

Andrew Clark is a music and arts journalist on *The Financial Times,* and a member of the editorial board of *Opera* magazine.

Della Couling writes on opera and theatre for *The Independent, The Financial Times, Opera Now* and various European newspapers and journals.

Massimo De Bernart, the conductor, studied at the Conservatories of Venice, Florence and Turin, at the Academy of Vienna and the Accademia Chigiana, Siena.

Nigel Douglas, tenor, has appeared throughout the world in a repertoire of over eighty principal tenor roles. He is also well known as a broadcaster and director, and as the author of two widely acclaimed books, *Legendary Voices* and *More Legendary Voices.*

Gordon French is an Australian television producer and London gallery owner.

Christina Grimandi, dancer, singer and actress, was born in Bologna and has worked in various professional shows throughout Europe, including playing Norma Desmond in the German production of *Sunset Boulevard.*

Paul Gruber, Executive Director, Program Development, The Metropolitan Opera Guild, New York.

Manfred Haedler has been dramaturg and editor at the Deutsche Staatsoper, Berlin, since 1978.

Kate Hardy is a former Deputy Editor of *Opera Now.*

The Earl of Harewood, KBE, was Managing Director of the English National Opera 1972-85, and Chairman 1986-95.

Peter Hill is the translator of the text from the German on pages 20, 22 and 124-125, and from the French on page 43.

David Hockney is an artist, set and costume designer, film maker, illustrator.

Bruce Johnston is the Rome correspondent for *The Daily Telegraph*.

Graeme Kay is Online Producer and Presenter BBC Radio 3; previously editor of *Opera Now*.

Vincenzo La Scola, tenor, is one of the foremost 'new voices' of his generation.

Bernard Levin is author, opera lover and columnist for *The Times*.

Jorge Listopad is a poet, writer, film producer, literary critic and Director of the Academy of Cinema and Theatre of Portugal.

Andrew Parrott is a conductor and musicologist.

Sir Georg Solti (1912-1997) was one of the 20th century's foremost conductors. During his long and distinguished career he was Music Director at the Royal Opera House, Covent Garden, 1961-71.

George C. Spelvin, theatre critic, New York.

Dame Joan Sutherland, 'La Stupenda', is the most renowned exponent of the art of bel canto.

Dr. Beat Unternährer is a banker, opera lover and singer.

Tunku Varadarajan is a correspondent on *The Times*.

Galina Vishnevskaya is an eminent Russian soprano.

While personal reminiscences, anecdotes and appraisals are signed, the introductions to the opera houses are not. These were provided by:

Stephenson B. Andrews Barcelona, Bayreuth, Brussels, Dresden, Lisbon, London, Madrid, Marseilles, Milan, Monaco, Montpellier, Moscow, Salzburg, Stuttgart, Vienna.

Della Couling Munich, Paris (Opéra Comique).

Manfred Haedler Berlin.

Kate Hardy Stockholm (Drottningholm).

Bruce Johnston Pesaro, Reggio Emilia, Venice.

Andras Kaldor Budapest, Geneva, Glyndebourne, Lyons, New York, Prague (Stavovské Divadlo), San Francisco, Stockholm (Kungliga Teatern), Sydney, Zurich.

Graeme Kay Paris (Palais Garnier), Prague (Národní Divadlo).

BARCELONA
GRAN TEATRE DEL LICEU

Creative planning and public subscription by a growing merchant class account for the opening of the Liceu in 1847. Architects Miguel Garriga i Roca and Josep Oriol Mestres designed the new theatre on an irregular urban lot. The same architects returned to rebuild after a devastating fire in 1861 destroyed most of the stage and auditorium. Shares were sold to raise the necessary funds for an even more luxurious theatre than the one which burned and many seats are still 'owned' by descendants of these original contributors. Queen Isabel II graciously assisted with the funding of the new theatre in the 1840s. When she refused to help in 1861, patrons 'voiced' their displeasure by reconstructing the auditorium without a Royal Box. The Renaissance façade of the original 1847 theatre, facing the prestigious Las Ramblas, is characterised by arches at every level and divided by pairs of engaged columns on the *piano nobile*.

The 18th century in Spain was known for a type of national operetta called the 'zarzuela', a style often compared to that of Gilbert and Sullivan, and when the theatre reopened in 1862 it was this form of opera which was experiencing a revival. The very distinctive zarzuela is regularly seen at the Liceu where it is a policy to produce at least one new Spanish opera each year. One, *Doña Francisquita* (1923) by Catalan composer Amadeo Vives, enjoys such popularity that it has become part of the repertory.

While the exterior of the Liceu has a somewhat simple yet strong feeling, the interior clearly shows a more elaborate French influence in style and plan, with various details

---

The architects: Miguel Garriga i Roca and Josep Oriol Mestres
The building: Opened 1847; fire 1861, reopened 1862; fire 1994, reopened 1999
Capacity: About 2500
Opening perfomance: Donizetti's *Anna Bolena*
World première: Balada's *Christobal Colón*, 1989
Notable appearance: Victoria de los Angeles, aged 16, as Mimi in Puccini's *La bohème*

13

from Louis XV through Art Nouveau. A red and gold horseshoe-shaped auditorium has a capacity for almost three thousand patrons with five levels of boxes, several with anterooms. The ceiling, like many of the reception rooms, incorporates murals set into gilded frames.

Although the Liceu opened on 4 April 1847, the first opera was not seen there until two weeks later with *Anna Bolena* by Donizetti, followed the next month by Verdi's *I due Foscari*. After reconstruction in 1862, the theatre reopened with *I Puritani* by Bellini.

The Liceu's initial reputation was as an 'Italian house', especially where Puccini was concerned (indeed even French operas performed at this time were sung in Italian). In the later part of the 19th century the focus was on Wagner. Eventually this evolved into a preference for Strauss, Debussy and a Russian/Slavonic repertoire.

Used as a pawn by both sides in the Spanish Civil War of the 1930s, the theatre reverted to private ownership in 1939 and hosted companies from Berlin and Frankfurt during World War II with a Mozart Festival in 1939 and a Wagner Festival in 1940.

The Liceu is the 'home' for some of the most important singers on the world stage today. Montserrat Caballé was awarded the Liceu's gold medal in 1954; other Barcelona natives include José Carreras and Giacomo Aragall, while Alfredo Kraus, from Las Palmas, trained there. Known as a venue for great singers and a generally unimaginative repertoire, the Liceu hosted the world première in 1989 of *Christóbal Colón* by Leonardo Balada with Caballé as Queen Isabel I and Carreras as a truly exceptional Columbus.

Julio Bravo

On 31 January 1994, flames devoured one of the most handsome of the world's opera houses, the Liceu of Barcelona. Five and a half years later, after a complete rebuilding of the interior, the Liceu opened again in October 1999.

A jewel of mid-19th century architecture, a place charged with evocative literary history, the Liceu is the city's cultural symbol. Barcelona is its 'owner', and a proud one at that.

The Liceu is part of the landscape of the city's most popular avenue, Las Ramblas, a pedestrian *via* with deep roots in Barcelona's psyche. There, by the newspaper kiosks, the cafés, the florists and the aviaries, rises the monumental façade of the Liceu.

Extraordinarily *señorial* and elegant, a reflection of the aspirations of Barcelona's commercial bourgeoisie, of a city which has always regarded the future with panache, the Teatre del Liceu opened its doors on 4 April 1847. Its full name was the Gran Teatre del Liceu de Isabel II, and had taken the architect Miguel Garriga i Roca only two years to build.

It was a busy first night; a symphony by José Melchor Comis was performed, as well as *Don Fernando de Antequera*, a drama by Ventura de la Vega. And there was more: the ballet *La Rondeña* by Josep Jurch and the cantata *Il regio imene* by Marià Obiols. Days later, Donizetti's first opera, *Anna Bolena*, was staged, to obvious civic joy. Yet barely fourteen years after its inauguration, the first tragedy occurred: a fire in the tailor's workshop destroyed the stage. There were no victims, and the theatre was able to reopen a year later, on 20 April 1862.

The Teatre del Liceu has lived to its city's rhythm like few other opera houses, forming part of Barcelona's social fabric from its very first day. The spectacle it provides is as much on stage, through which passed the best singers and operas, as in the Liceu's passageways and boxes, where the elegant Catalan bourgeoisie seems permanently to nest. To keep a box at the Liceu is an enormous status symbol, and is inherited by sons from fathers. Business deals are done in the boxes, and marriages arranged.

Barcelona's history cannot be told without mentioning the Liceu, and Spanish and Catalan literature is replete with references to it. Its symbolism is so strong that it was once the scene of a politically-motivated attack: on 7 September 1893 the anarchist Santiago Salvador lobbed two bombs into the circle. One failed to explode, the other killed twenty people.

For the record, Rossini's *William Tell* was to have been performed that night.

15

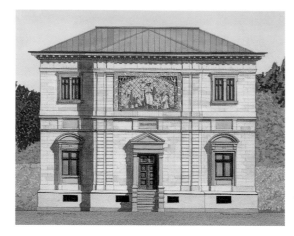

Haus Wahnfried,
Wagner's home in
Bayreuth, now a museum

BAYREUTH
FESTSPIELHAUS

What was originally constructed as a temporary theatre has proved to be one of the most visually interesting and acoustically superb opera houses to be found anywhere. While travelling through Germany in search of a suitable home for his *Ring* cycle, composer Richard Wagner became enchanted with Bayreuth. In 1872 he commissioned Leipzig architect Otto Brückwald to draw up the plans for an opera house funded by a series of concerts. When these failed to raise as much as hoped, necessity dictated the style incorporating the cheapest possible materials, namely brick and wood. The building realised has stood the test of time and speaks well for itself.

The interior was modelled along the lines of an enclosed classical amphitheatre. Seating for over 1,800 is arranged on a single raked level, unencumbered with boxes, loges or galleries. Wagner himself was primarily responsible for the acoustics, assisted by the engineer Karl Brandt. The most innovative aspect of his design was a deep, stepped orchestra pit with curved wooden canopy or cowl hiding the conductor and players, and enabling the instruments to be deflected back to combine with the voices on stage before filtering to the audience.

The house and the first Wagner festival was inaugurated in 1876 with the *Ring* cycle conducted by Hans Richter. Since that time the Festspielhaus has understandably been the venue for some of the most important performances of Wagner's *oeuvre*. *Parsifal*, which was conceived for the Bayreuth audience, had its début here in 1882, conducted by Wagner. He died the following year. The opera house still serves as the home of the annual Bayreuth Festival.

Bernard Levin

Richard Wagner's Festspielhaus is approached by a hill. A mild hill, but a hill nevertheless. It would be going too far if we said that the hill was an emblem – a warning

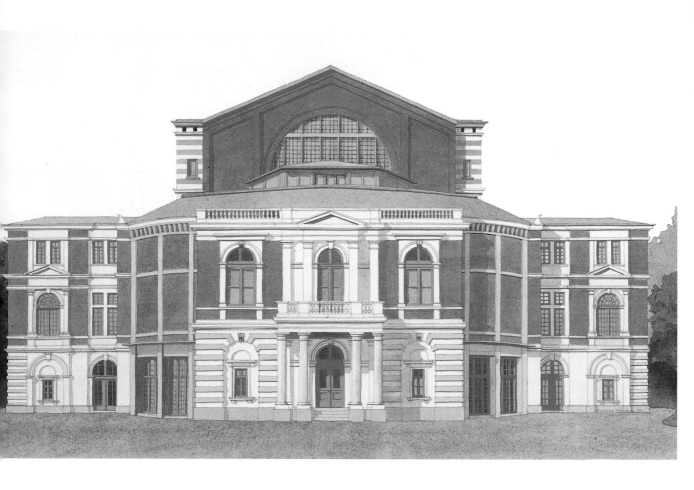

that what we are to see and hear is not for the faint-hearts. Yet when we come down the hill (which is many, many hours later) we feel that we have endured a great test, and passed it. And so we have.

When we come to the top of that mild hill (which, incidentally, is lavishly strewn with flowers on both sides) we see first a flag fluttering in the breeze. This flag has nothing on it but the letter W. That W stands for Wagner, just in case the newcomer thinks that it is all about Beethoven or Mozart. Now, for at least a week, and usually more, we will hear and see and think of one man and his genius.

We have got our breath back, and we can now study the very remarkable building that

The architects: Otto Brückwald and Richard Wagner
The building: Opened 1876
Capacity: About 1800
Opening perfomances: Wagner's *Ring* cycle
World première: Wagner's *Parsifal*, 1882
Notable appearances: The audience for the opening in 1876 included Liszt, Greig, Bruckner, Mahler, Tchaikovsky, Saint-Saens, Nietzsche, Tolstoy, Kaiser Wilhelm I of Prussia, and King Ludwig II of Bavaria

stands before us. It is huge, but not bright – it is indeed subfusc, and that is no accident. We are here, not to admire the surely unique building, though whole studies have been written about it, but to get into the proper mood for what is to come. And indeed there is much chatter on the mighty terrace before the trumpeters sound the warning to go in, but in all that chatter there is very little laughter. Wagner is serious, and those who come to hear him know it.

Wagner's music is not like any other's. It is truly *sui generis*, and there are few, very few, who can take Wagner and leave him; love him or hate him is the flag that flies in all our hearts when we are contemplating Wagner. Curiously, I came to Wagner without hearing a single note of his music. I read, as a schoolboy, Bernard Shaw's *The Perfect Wagnerite*, and although I had no idea of what or who Wagner was, I was fired with the passion of Shaw's writing. Moreover, there were no gramophone records – in those days, records ran for only four-and-a-half minutes, which precluded Wagner. So I had to wait for Proms; there had been no Wagner during the war, and the first sound of his music came from a *pot-pourri* of his works. The rest you know, or at least if you know me.

What is it that makes slaves of Wagner, and passionately love his chains? I do not know, and fear to find out. For Wagner demands total subjection; we even put up with the appalling seats in the Festspielhaus – they dig into our backs, we have to twist our knees into dreadful shapes, and if ever the two fire-engines which stand always beside the building were needed, I do believe that we would be still arguing about the tenor in the second act while the flames leaped into the sky.

Sometimes, I think I will give up Wagner entirely. But I lie; when those subterranean notes float out at the beginning of *Das Rheingold*, I am once more Richard Wagner's slave. And loving it!

BAYREUTH
MARKGRÄFLICHES OPERNHAUS

This exquisite jewel of an opera house was built for Wilhelmina, Margravine of Bayreuth and sister of Frederick the Great of Prussia, in 1745-8. The stone façade has giant-order Corinthian columns set *en antis* on the first floor above a rusticated stone ground floor with three arched doors. The architect, Frenchman Joseph Saint-Pierre, used segmented-arch windows and Corinthian pilasters to finish the side bays. A balustrade supporting full-size figures runs along the top of the façade in front of a hipped roof.

Inside, Italian interior designer Giuseppe Galli-Bibiena created a Baroque hall in blue-green and gold. Bell-shaped, a trademark of this Italian family renowned for operatic design, the auditorium can accommodate only about five hundred in three loge levels. For obvious reasons, there is an ornate box surrounded by columns and topped with a canopy. The box often served as a counter-attraction almost as riveting as the stage it faced. With hardly a division between the stage and the audience, the interior is

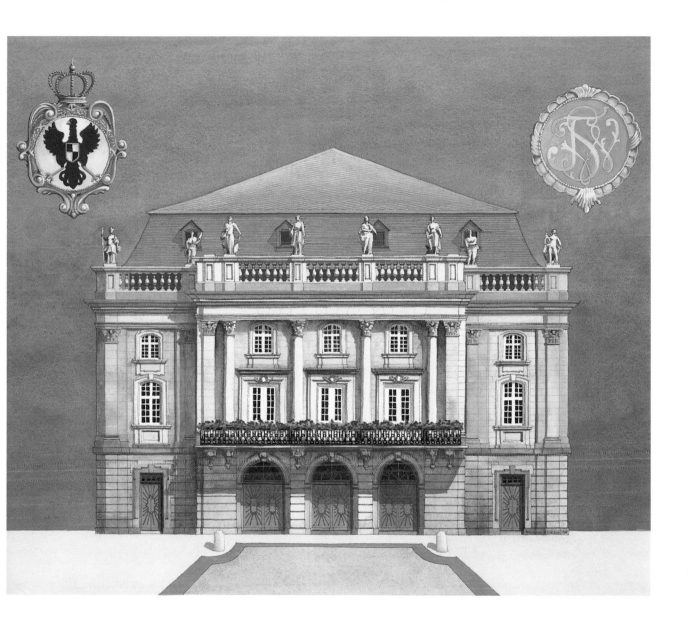

occasionally lit by hundreds of candles, when the gilded decoration shines and glimmers.

Fortunately, given the history of Germany, neither bombs nor politicians have altered this remarkable structure in nearly 250 years.

Today the opera house is regularly used and much loved, with the Bavarian State Opera presenting an annual spring festival.

The architect: Joseph Saint-Pierre
The building: Opened 1748, built for Wilhelmina, Margravine of Bayreuth
Capacity: About 520

BERLIN
DEUTSCHE STAATSOPER

In 1992 the Staatsoper Unter den Linden celebrated its 250th anniversary. Originally conceived as Frederick the Great's Royal Opera House, it is Berlin's oldest theatrical building and one of the world's most beautiful opera houses. Built between 1741 and 1743 by Georg Wenzeslaus von Knobelsdorff, it opened on 7 December 1742, still only part complete, with a performance of Carl Heinrich Graun's *Cesare e Cleopatre*. Until 1801, the house remained the exclusive preserve of the royal court and invited guests, and it was only in 1807, after the merger of the royal opera and the Nationaltheater as the Königliche Schauspiele (Royal Theatrical Spectacles) that its doors were opened to the citizens of Berlin and the German opera.

Pinnacles of Berlin's operatic history in the 19th century include the première of Weber's *Der Freischütz* at Schinkel's new Schauspielhaus on Gendermenmarkt in 1821, the work of Gasparo Spontini and Giacomo Meyerbeer as directors of music, and of Karl Friedrich Schinkel as stage designer at Unter den Linden. One of the most beautiful and joyous works of the German operatic repertoire, Otto Nicolai's *The Merry Wives of Windsor,* was first performed at Unter den Linden, with the composer conducting, in 1849.

Towards the end of the 19th century, after several decades dominated more by international singing stars than by truly first-class standards, the opera house rose to world prominence under such conductors as Joseph Sucher, Felix Weingartner and Karl Muck, and later particularly Richard Strauss and Leo Blech.

After 1918 and the end of Kaiser Wilhelm II's empire, the Unter den Linden opera house focused more and more on contemporary composers, writing another chapter of operatic history with the world première of *Wozzeck* conducted by Erich Kleiber.

This steady development was brought to an abrupt halt when the National Socialists came to power, with many leading artists such as the conductors Erich Kleiber, Otto Klemperer and Leo Blech fleeing into exile. However, thanks to the diplomatic aplomb of the then general manager Heinz Tietjen, Unter den Linden was able to maintain its accustomed high standards. During World War II, Knobelsdorff's opera

The architect: Georg Wenzeslaus von Knobelsdorff
The building: Opened 1742; fire 1843, reopened 1844; bomb damage 1945, reconstructed by 1955
Capacity: About 1400
Opening perfomance: Graun's *Cesare e Cleopatre*
World première: Weber's *Der Freischutz*, 1821

house was destroyed by bombs in 1941, then rapidly rebuilt. Closed for public operatic performances in 1944 by Goebbel's 'total war', it was destroyed again in 1945. After the end of the war, the company quickly reassembled, giving performances at the Admiral's Palace which had survived the war virtually unscathed.

The beautiful Unter den Linden opera house was rebuilt between 1952 and 1955, under the guidance of the architect Richard Paulick. On 4 September 1955, it reopened with Wagner's *Die Meistersinger von Nürnberg* – musical direction by Franz Konwitschny and stage design by general manager Max Burghardt. During the years that followed, in spite of the building of the Berlin Wall in 1961 and the resulting restrictions, the State Opera House retained its international reputation and built up an extensive repertoire of German classics and romantic pieces, as well as new work and international opera and ballet classics under general managers Pischner and Rimkus.

Since the fall of the Berlin Wall in 1989, and especially since the reunification of the two Germanys in 1990, the Staatsoper Unter den Linden again sees itself as a full member of the European operatic establishment. The present artistic director, the conductor Daniel Barenboim, has been invited to take control of both the Staatsoper and the Deutsche Oper if they merge, but as we go to press the matter is unresolved.

At the Staatsoper, Barenboim has continued the 250-year history of the opera house and seeks to bring the people of Berlin and their guests from all over the world all the riches of the German and European operatic and balletic tradition, including contemporary work, in interpretations of the highest calibre.

Manfred Haedler

With rich traditions that few other musical theatres in Germany can match, the State Opera House has a significant place in operatic history. When Frederick the Great commanded his master architect Knobelsdorff to build the opera house on Unter den Linden, he was pursuing an ambitious goal: his 'enchanted castle', as he described the opera house, was to be the foundation stone of Prussia's cultural metropolis. A central element of the architectural ensemble that is the 'Forum Friderizianum' in the heart of Berlin and which, more than any other part of the city, embodies his vision for the (cultural) capital of Prussia, the State Opera House is the musical focus of Berlin.

Its quality is defined in the dialectic of tradition and innovation, in a continuing exploration and reworking of the operatic *oeuvre* of three centuries. A particular emphasis, apart from the key works of European operatic tradition, are operas of the pre-Mozartian era, making use of historical staging practices to produce living performances true to the spirit of the time. In keeping with the flowering of innovative musical theatre in the 21st century, Unter den Linden's staging of modern classics is central to its programming which encompasses the seminal works of the 21st century, as well as an exploration of the frontiers of contemporary opera through world premières.

The basic principle informing the work of the State Opera under the artistic direction of Daniel Barenboim is to give equal treatment to all the disciplines that contribute to the total work of art. Accordingly, the stage design and musical direction are of the same superlative quality. The *stagione,* or 'series' principle, which determines the structure of the repertoire, makes it possible to stage individual productions with permanent ensembles (casting guest artists and soloists drawn from the powerful company of young singers) and optimal conditions for scheduling rehearsals, without restricting the diversity of the programme. An annual opera festival has been inaugurated.

The creative interplay of tradition and innovation also determines the artistic direction of the State Opera Ballet, a highly trained classical company with internationally respected soloists, who are as familiar with the great romantic and classical ballets as they are with modern pieces, some of them choreographed especially for the company.

In the Berlin State Symphony, Unter den Linden has a superb orchestra rich in tradition which offers its own exciting and varied concert programme alongside the opera and ballet productions. The State Opera House complements its programme with symphony concerts, evenings of Lieder and chamber music, as well as less conventional presentations such as puppet theatre and film seasons, often tying in with the current opera and ballet productions.

BRUSSELS
THÉÂTRE ROYAL DE LA MONNAIE

During the middle ages the site of the theatre was occupied by the royal mint. When Maximilian-Emanuel of Bavaria decreed that a 'grand theatre' be erected in the square, the first Théâtre de la Monnaie was built in 1700. In 1810 when Napoleon visited Brussels with the Empress Marie-Louise, they were so disturbed by the poor state of the theatre that they pledged a new opera house. The present building dates from 1817 and was designed by the Parisian Neo-Classical architect Damesne. The second Théâtre de la Monnaie was inaugurated on 25 May 1819 with Grétry's *La caravane du Caire*.

La Monnaie set the scene which prompted the creation of modern-day Belgium. In August 1830 there was a special performance of Auber's *La muette de Portici* which focuses on events surrounding the uprising of the Neapolitans against their Spanish oppressors in 1647. Ruled by William I of Orange, Belgium was steeped in political unrest at the time and the duet 'Amour sacré de la patrie' provoked the audience to storm from the theatre and join the despondent crowds in the Place de la Monnaie. Within six weeks the constitutional monarchy was born and William I was replaced by Prince Leopold of Saxe-Coburg who became Leopold I, King of Belgium.

During preparations for a performance of Meyerbeer's *Le prophéte* in 1855, fire broke out on stage and quickly spread through the theatre leaving only Damesne's shell. The interior was redesigned in the Louis XVI style by the French architect Joseph Poelaert. The impressive Ionic portico was added at this time with a pediment sculpture by Eugène Simonis entitled, 'L'Harmonie des Passions Humaines'. The splendid 'new' opera house opened on 23 March 1856 with Halévy's comic opera *Jaguarita l'Indienne*.

The late 19th century was the golden age for La Monnaie, boasting a string of world premières: Lecocq's *La fille de Madame Angot* (1872) and *Giroflé-Girofla* (1874), Massenet's *Hérodiade* (1881), Reyer's *Sigurd* (1884) and *Salammbô* (1890), Chabrier's *Gwendoline* (1886), Godard's *Jocelyn* (1888) and Leroux's *Evangeline* (1895). In 1887 the stage was graced by the performance of Nellie Melba as Gilda in Verdi's *Rigoletto*. Enrico Caruso sang Rodolfo in Puccini's *La bohème* in 1910.

Artists refused to perform during the German occupation of Belgium in World War I. The Monnaie company reopened in 1918 and competed well with such houses as La Scala and the Paris Opéra in recognition and quality of performances. During the 1920s the opera house saw the premières of Milhaud's *Les malheurs d'Orphée* (1926), Honegger's *Antigone* (1927) and Prokofiev's *The Gambler* (1929).

In the 1950s the theatre was condemned as a fire risk, and the application for a 'special dispensation' (due to lack of funds for necessary improvements) stalled closure for another twenty-five years.

However, in 1985 there was no choice but to close. Sixteen months later a new foyer and rehearsal room were created, reception areas and corridors were refurbished and many interior spaces designed to incorporate the work of contemporary international artists. The auditorium has a capacity of just over 1,100. Today La Monnaie also hosts ballet and symphony performances. Generous government support and innovative administration have made it one of the most envied houses in Europe.

The architect: Louis Damesne
The building: Opened 1819; fire 1855, reopened 1856
Capacity: About 1100
Opening perfomance: Grétry's *La caravane du Caire*
World première: Lecocqu's *Giroflé-Girofla*, 1874

BUDAPEST
MAGYAR ÁLLAMI OPERÁHAZ

Encouraged by the pianist-composer Ferenc Liszt and the composer-conductor Ferenc Erkel, a committee was set up in 1872 to build an opera house in Budapest. Opera has been enjoyed in Hungary for some two hundred years; in noble houses to begin with, then in theatres in the capital and the provinces.

The purpose-built opera house was designed by Miklos Ybl; construction started in 1875 and, using only Hungarian craftsmen and artists, nine years later the Austro-Hungarian Emperor Franz-Joseph opened the Royal Hungarian Opera House. The ceremonial opening performances of selections from two Hungarian operas, *Bánk bán* and *Hunyadi László,* was followed by the first act of *Lohengrin.*

After the pomp of the royal opening, the reality of over-extended budgets meant slow progress and pricey tickets. In 1888 Gustav Mahler became director for three years and with István Kerner raised the musical standards and invited foreign performers, to encourage Hungarian singers. In 1912 Sandor Henesi became director and with the Italian conductor Egisto Tango set about building up the repertoire. Two first performances – Bartók's ballet

The Wooden Prince and opera *Duke Bluebeard's Castle* – were given before World War I intervened.

The 1920s and 1930s in Hungary, as in all Europe, were times of artistic innovation and excitement. The conductor Sergio Failoni continued the Italian repertoire and the introduction of young, talented conductors like János Ferencsik and György Solti (George Solti) who conducted *Le nozze di Figaro* in 1938. The seasons were illuminated by guest appearances by the most illustrious names of the music world, with Thomas Beecham, Bruno Walter, Herbert von Karajan conducting and Benjamino Gigli singing with Hungarian performers who were also reaching international standards.

World War II devastated the city; during the siege of Budapest the cellars of the opera house were used as an air raid shelter for most of the company, among them the family of composer Zoltán Kodály.

The radical change of system following the Soviet invasion of Hungary in 1956 gave the people access to culture and opera within the restrictions of Communism. The price to pay was the banning of politically incorrect works and the staging of socialist operas. Nevertheless, the popularity of opera grew and a second theatre was given to the company for

performances of opera and operetta. In 1980 the opera house closed for reconstruction and reopened in 1984 to a new world, ready to face up to the challenges and changes all over central Europe.

The architect: Miklos Ybl
The building: Opened 1884 with innovative hydraulic stage machinery; closed 1944, reopened after war; restored to original glory in the 1980s
Capacity: About 1260
Opening perfomances: Act I of Wagner's *Lohengrin* and selections from Hungarian operas
World première: Bartok's *Bluebeard's Castle*, 1918

Miklos Borsa

Some fifteen years ago I wrote a book *The Unknown Opera House* (published in Hungarian and sold out by now). The title may be misleading as the Budapest opera house is a well-known, well-respected and honoured house of the art of opera and ballet. My story is not about the music, the musicians, the singers or the dancers, but about the building, the splendid walls, the genius of its architect Miklos Ybl and of the wondrous machinery to create the stage illusions.

The reader will know that Gustav Mahler was director at the end of the 19th century, that Rudolf Nureyev brought the house to its feet with thunderous applause, and that the company prepares for more than four hundred performances a year from its wide repertoire. A separate chapter, could be written about the lives of the many eminent conductors who started their careers here and who, following the dictum of Ferenc Liszt that 'the artist's home is the whole wide world', left Budapest for wider horizons, among them Antal Doráti, Ferenc Fricsay, István Kertész, János Kulka, Jenö (Eugène) Ormándy and György Solti. I could have written about the two great Hungarian composers of the 20th century, Béla Bartók and Zoltán Kodály, whose many operas were premièred here, and of Aurél Miloss who took Bartók's ballet *The Miraculous Mandarin* around the world.

My unknown opera house is not about these great performers, but about the building itself which, since its opening days, has contained the pure artistry of the performances and also provided home and warmth and demanded attention and humility from all those within. It was due to a sad turn of events that the Budapest opera house was for a time the most modern building of its type. The building work was but half-way complete when the Ring Theatre in Vienna burned down with considerable loss of life. Following this tragic accident, safety regulations for theatres were greatly improved and the first theatre to comply was the Budapest opera house; it boasted the first safety/iron curtain

to separate the stage from the auditorium, the first sprinkler system over the stage and – difficult to believe nowadays – the first theatre to have escape doors, opening outwards in the direction of escape.

The most interesting and innovative development was the new stage machinery. The backstage of most theatres was usually built of timber, according to tradition rooted in shipbuilding and sailing ships. The theatre as a place for performances emerged from entertainments organised, usually for royal events, in large halls in palaces. The requirement to hoist large painted canvas backgrounds for a performance needed experts, and who knew better to raise canvas aloft than sailors? This traditional practice is still seen in some theatres.

But all the old ways were changed in Budapest. The stage was built of iron and moved by water – neither will burn. This was the first stage in the world to be moved by hydraulic power. It

was an experiment and few had much faith in its success. As it was, the stage machinery lasted nearly one hundred years, working silently and almost without fault. It was a fantastic sight under the stage, the cobweb of cast iron piping, huge water storage tanks dwarfing the operators, the machinery looking like an illustration to one of Jules Verne's adventures.

Even such an engineering feat grows old and defects begin to appear; the whole system was starting to show its age. Before the old machinery was dismantled I talked to the old hands who lived for many years under the stage tending and caring for the equipment. These conversations revealed many secrets: old thunder and wind machines, wonderful statues, and much of the old timber equipment, hidden in dark corners of the loft, unused for years but nevertheless part of the soul of the house. It was at this time of change and renewal that I started to collect material for *The Unknown Opera House*.

The Budapest opera house, after a three-year programme of renewal, reopened on 21 September 1984, exactly one hundred years after its opening. I hope that all the beauty and spirit within the old walls has been preserved for generations to come, and that the opera house will continue into the 21st century to nourish and guard the tradition of Hungarian opera.

DRESDEN
STAATSOPER

More often known as the Semperoper, the State Opera in Dresden is a magnificent tribute to its architect Gottfried Semper, to the history of German opera and to one building's ability to rebound in the face of repeated adversity. Its position on the west side of the Theaterplatz, opposite the Royal Palace, confirms its original importance to a ruling house that had maintained a keen interest in the arts for over a century. First opening in 1841 as the Royal Saxon Opera House, this was one of the earliest purpose-built theatres in which the function of the interior dictated the shape of the exterior, and hosted all forms of stage productions before being devoted exclusively to opera in this century. Carl Maria von Weber's *Euryanthe* was the first opera performed in the new theatre.

In 1843, Richard Wagner was made Kapellmeister a year after the première of *Rienzi* (1842). Soon after his appointment, the house premièred two other works by Wagner: *Der fliegende Holländer* (1843) and *Tannhäuser* (1845). Due to revolutionary political activity, in

1849 Wagner found it necessary to leave Dresden for Switzerland where he lived for thirteen years, returning only after he was pardoned.

Semper's original building burned down in 1869, and after much debate, the opera house was rebuilt on the site, duplicating his 1841 design.

During the first four decades of this century, the Semperoper (officially renamed the Staatsoper in 1918) was the venue which gave Richard Strauss international fame with such premières as *Salome* (1905), *Der Rosenkavalier* (1911), *Die Ägyptische Helena* (1928), and *Daphne* (1938).

As was the case with most of Dresden, the Semperoper was gutted by Allied saturation bombing in 1945. Only the walls remained. Although a temporary roof was put into place and there was much discussion about building a modern opera house within the shell, nothing was done to rebuild the theatre until 1975 when the original architectural drawings were discovered in Vienna. Ten painstaking years were required to return the Semperoper to its original 19th-century glory and the theatre reopened on 13 February 1985, exactly forty years after the destruction. *Der Freischütz* was the opera chosen to reopen the opera house in 1985, an acknowledgement of Carl

Maria von Weber's numerous contributions to Dresden's operatic history in the first quarter of the 19th century.

The beautiful 'new' auditorium is known for outstanding acoustics and state-of-the-art technology. All operas are performed in German to make them accessible to local audiences and the repertoire is heavily weighted towards the important 'Dresden' composers of Weber, Wagner and Strauss. This policy of opera being 'by and in' the German language demonstrates how the people of Dresden have taken their rich operatic history, founded almost exclusively in the early 18th-century from Italian roots, and made it representative of their own culture.

The architect: Gottfried Semper
The building: Opened 1841; fire 1869, reopened 1878; bomb damage 1945, reopened 1985
Capacity: About 1200
World première: Richard Strauss's *Salome,* 1905

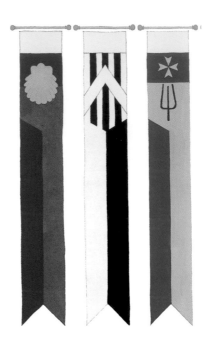

GENEVA
GRAND THÉÂTRE

The Grand Théâtre (named in 1910) was originally opened in 1879 with Rossini's *Guillaume Tell*, the Swiss patriotic opera. Located in the old town next to the museum, *conservatoire* and the university, the opera house is a grand piece of architecture designed for grand occasions as befits such a wealthy city. Following a fire in 1951 the interior of the theatre was reconstructed with particular attention paid to the stage and orchestra pit which were equipped with the latest machinery and adjustable to the size required. Generous subscriptions and an annual budget from the city for the maintenance of the building is a rare luxury enjoyed by the Grand Théâtre.

The refurbished house opened in December 1962 with a production of Verdi's *Don Carlos* in the original French version. Herbert Graf was appointed director in 1965 and set the standard of innovative productions with the staging of Mozart's *Die Zauberflöte* designed by Oscar Kokoschka and the revival of many unfamiliar works.

In 1973 Jean-Claude Riber followed as director and took responsibility for producing much of the repertoire himself. In 1980 he was succeeded by Hugues Gall, from the Paris Opéra, whose guiding principle was to treat each production separately, choosing stage director, designer and conductor to suit each opera. Maurice Béjart's productions

of *Don Giovanni* and *Salome*, the première productions of Rolf Liebermann's *La forêt* and Girolamo Arrigo's *Il ritorno di Casanova,* and Ken Russell directing *L'Italiana in Algeri* are but a few examples of Gall's philosophy at work.

The Grand Théâtre stages eight operas and two ballets a season, each receiving between six and twelve performances. This *stagione* system allows a decent period for rehearsals and the same cast to stay with the production from first to last performance. Although star conductors or singers are seldom invited, the Grand Théâtre consistently pleases its audience of subscribers, international visitors, young opera lovers, and university students.

The architect: Jacques-Elysée Goss
The building: Opened 1879; fire 1951, reopened 1962
Capacity: About 1500
Opening perfomance: Rossini's *William Tell*
World premières: Arrigo's *Il Ritorno di Casanova*, 1985; Liebermann's *La Forêt*, 1987

Andrew Clark

It would be wrong to say the Grand Théâtre has the status of a metropolitan opera house – but equally misguided to say it is provincial. It lies somewhere in between. You will see well-made productions, as befits a house which has stuck to the *stagione* principle. You will hear good singers, especially young Americans who have begun to make their way in Europe. But don't expect star casting or a sense of occasion. That is not what the Grand Théâtre is about.

Geneva may be one of the great international meeting places, but it is a small city, and it does not lavish money on its opera season. Whoever is in charge at the Grand Théâtre learns to be resourceful. There will be a couple of co-productions, a handful done on the cheap, and one or two opulent shows to prove Geneva knows how to do things in style.

Whatever happens on stage, polite applause is guaranteed. The Grand Théâtre's audiences are not rabid culture-vultures, intent on discussing the finer points of producer X's Marxist interpretaion of *La bohème*. They may be cosmopolitan – a mix of diplomats and professionals, young and old, locals and tourists – and like everyone in French-speaking Switzerland, they may aspire to *le style français*; but in the operatic taste they are old-fashioned Calvinists. Something familiar and tuneful will do nicely, thank you.

For Geneva's matrons, dressed in their fading fur coats, an opera subscription is *de rigueur;* you can hear them packing away their spectacles and programme books long before the curtain comes down. But there is also an element of public service about the Grand Théâtre: prices are low, and on the few evenings when a non-subscription audience fills the house, the dynamics between stage and public liven up.

The auditorium, rebuilt after a fire in 1951, is a bit modern-vulgar, but the seats are comfortable and the sight-lines good. It is backed by the original public rooms and staircases, now restored to their former splendour and boasting the spaciousness of a 19th century municipal theatre proud of its function – not tucked away, as in British cities, in side streets.

It is not a theatre of ghosts, but it has a past to be proud of. This is where Ansermet conducted *Pelléas* and *Pénélope,* where Kokoschka designed *Die Zauberflöte,* where Hugues Gall spent fifteen productive years (1980-95) before taking on the Bastille in Paris. Gall put Geneva on the international opera map, and we who witnessed those years will be forever in his debt. We heard Tatiana Troyanos's incomparable Giulio Cesare, Ruggero Raimondi's one-and-only Falstaff, Marie McLaughlin's angelic Blanche (*Carmélites*), Samuel Ramey's devil incarnate in operas by Gounod and Boito, Elizabeth Connell's fearless Odabella. There was a Britten cycle, and much innovative staging.

What those halcyon years proved is that an opera house can be much more than bricks and mortar. Its personality – the stuff, the smell, the sense of excitement that sticks in our memory, however distant in time or place we may be – derives from the people who work there, and the art they create in a moment of time.

GLYNDEBOURNE
FESTIVAL OPERA

The Glyndebourne Festival was founded in 1934 by John Christie and his wife, the singer Audrey Mildmay. The first Artistic Directors were the conductor Fritz Busch and the director Carl Ebert. The Festival opened with a short season of two Mozart operas produced in the theatre built specially for the purpose at the Christie's home in the Sussex countryside. The success of the first season impressed sceptical critics and audiences alike.

These first performances established the standards Glyndebourne was to follow: attention to detail, quality of the orchestra, and singers selected on merit and suitability for the part, and ability to act.

The British professional première of Verdi's *Macbeth* was given in 1938, the first year that operas other than those by Mozart were given, and by the following year thirty-eight performances were given in the enlarged theatre. By the time war closed the theatre, the Glyndebourne Festival Opera was firmly established.

Performances at Glyndebourne were resumed in 1946/7. In 1952, first the Glyndebourne Festival Society and then the Glyndebourne Arts Trust were formed to relieve the Christie family of the financial burden and ensure the future of Glyndebourne. Moran Caplat took over as General Manager from Rudolf Bing in 1948 when the latter left for the Metropolitan Opera in New York, and Gunther Rennert followed Carl Ebert as Artistic Director in 1960. George Christie succeeded his father as chairman of Glyndebourne Productions Ltd. in 1959.

The essential ethos of Glyndebourne was maintained by the introduction of new operas, the work of conductor Vittorio Gui in Rossini's comedies and director Peter Hall with Mozart's Da Ponte operas, and by imaginative stagings and invitations to artists like David Hockney with his brilliant designs for *The Rake's Progress*. Glyndebourne Touring Opera was formed in 1968 to take productions to wider audiences and encourage and educate younger performers.

Mozart, Richard Strauss and Rossini have remained specialities of the house, which has also played host to a number of important premières, including Maw's *The Rising of the*

Moon, Osborne's *The Electrification of the Soviet Union*, Tippett's *New Year* and Birtwistle's *The Second Mrs Kong*.

The house closed at the end of the 1992 season to make way for a new theatre on the site of the old one. Built of hand-made bricks, the horseshoe shape of the auditorium is reflected in the circular lead-covered roof. The interior is all salvaged pitch pine, with curved surfaces everywhere for balanced acoustics. The new theatre opened on time and within budget, a feat of operatic proportions, on 28 May 1994 with Mozart's *Le nozze di Figaro* — exactly sixty years after the first production in the original theatre.

The architect: Michael Hopkins, 1994
The building: Opened 1934; purpose-built house opened 1994
Capacity: About 1200
Opening perfomances: Mozart's *The Marriage of Figaro,* 1934 and 1994
World premières: Britten's *The Rape of Lucretia,* 1946; Henze's *Elegy for Young Lovers,* 1961
Notable appearance: Kathleen Ferrier débuted in the *The Rape of Lucretia,* 1946

David Hockney

At the time of Glyndebourne's invitation to design *The Rake's Progress* I had not been doing much painting because I was trying to teach myself to draw better. I would spend two or three days working on a figure scrutinising it carefully. I thought this would improve my drawing because my eyes would see more.

'I had only a general idea of what an opera production might involve. I knew those at Covent Garden were usually more costly than ordinary theatre productions. The only thing I had done in the theatre, *Ubu Roi*, was very simply conceived, because it suited the work. Even though I told the Glyndebourne people I didn't really think I knew enough to do the job, they convinced me I did.

'I realised they expected me simply to make eight or nine drawings of the scenes and hand them over. They would then interpret these and make them into sets. So I started making a few drawings.

'Mo McDermott, a friend who worked for me then a bit, had also worked for a stage designer in London. He told me not just to do drawings because the result on stage might not look exactly as I wanted it to. I realised that working with something as stylised as opera, you must control how everything looks. You must design the production in three dimensions. I decided to make scale models of the sets.'

Hockney had long been fascinated by Hogarth's engravings on the Rake theme and those for 'Marriage à la Mode'. Intrigued with the precision of the crosshatching technique so prominent in these prints, he decided to apply similar patterning in exaggerated scale to all architectural elements and costumes in the production. That style is particularly expressive of the jagged, linear character of Stravinsky's music. Using the hallmark of 18th century engraving was consistent with the composer's own concept of the production. 'Stravinsky's music was a pastiche of Mozart's, and my design was a pastiche of Hogarth's', says Hockney.

'The misadventures of the Rake have no literary ancestry: we know it through Hogarth's eyes. . . To any English art student, William Hogarth is a great artist. It always seemed to me that he had a very human eye. He understood mankind's follies and had a soft spot for them, but his work also shows a certain delight in condemning low life.

'When the Rake is first seen in my two-colour prints, he is a vivid personality, but little by little he loses this quality. For the last scene, in Bedlam, I did a drawing of a faceless figure, then made a stamp of it that I impressed on the etching plate five times. You see five faceless people in the madhouse, but you can't tell which one the Rake is.'

In contrast to this very subjective conception of the Rake theme, Hockney made the designs for Glyndebourne hard-edged, finely detailed and calculated to enhance every aspect of the story. He incorporated these into models which he conceived of as three-dimensional drawings. He recalls showing them for the first time to the Glyndebourne staff in London.

'Everyone who was going to be involved with the production was there – the producers, the prop people, the lighting man. They were totally amazed when they saw the designs. They were expecting to see drawings, but I had made a model for almost every set. What I didn't know at the time was that some of them thought my ideas wouldn't work.

'I was concerned about the crosshatching too, so I decided to go to Glyndebourne and test my idea. We made lots of samples of crosshatchings in different sizes, and hung them up on the stage. I sat at the back of the theatre with binoculars, deciding what the scale should be. If it was done too small, it would look like a solid colour. If it was too big, it would look like a checkerboard – and that would be ridiculous. So I made some calculations and came up with the exact size.

'I think I arrived at the colour for the sets this way. Crosshatching is a graphic technique that

normally is done with a single colour. But then, I thought, we don't want to do it all in black and white. We have to use some coloured lines; so I simply chose what would have been standard printing colours in the 18th century. I bought good German inks: red, blue, green and black. There are no other colours in the design. I used colours in *The Rake* mainly as decorative elements. They are essentially tints.

'Where do you think I got the idea to use graffiti in the Bedlam scene? From Hogarth again, of course. I suddenly realised that in his Bedlam drawing, one of the madmen is scribbling a map of the world on the wall. Then I thought about what the walls of Bedlam must have been covered with and decided that in the 18th century the graffiti wouldn't have been political; probably it was mostly intellectual.'

The freedom of working on the Stravinsky opera encouraged Hockney to draw more adventurously again.

LISBON
TEATRO NACIONAL DE SÃO CARLOS

Italian opera had been the norm in Lisbon since the early 18th century, featuring such composers as Leo, Caldara and Carvalho. Even the first opera by Portuguese composer Francisco Almeida – *La pazienza di Socrate* – was performed in Italian. A magnificent opera house, the Teatro dos Pacos da Ribeira, opened in 1755 with *Alessandro nell'Indie* by David Perez. Unfortunately the theatre, said to be the most sumptuous to be found anywhere in Europe, was destroyed in the devastating earthquake of the same year. For the next few decades opera in Lisbon was performed at various theatres.

Diamond and tobacco merchants, wealthy from Portugal's business dealings in Brazil, gave the people of Lisbon a beautiful new opera house in 1792. In less than seven months, Italian-trained architect Jose Da Costa e Silva built a most opulent Neo-Classical style building based on the San Carlo opera house in Naples. The rusticated ground floor supports a stuccoed first floor with classical ornament. The three arches on the ground floor and the Doric-order columns above are characteristic of Palladio's rural structures in the Veneto. The whole composition retains the simple, elegant, well-established effect the benefactors wanted to achieve. Throughout the 19th century the new opera house was a prominent centre for Italian and Portuguese opera, often part of the plan for most of the finest singers in Europe.

On entering one is greeted with a veritable explosion of gold filigree complemented with soft shades of pale green, rose and parchment. Italian interior designers Apiani and Mazzoneschi fitted out the elaborate Royal Box that dominates and divides the three levels of loges, rising right up to the gallery. The oval-shaped auditorium has a capacity of just under 1,200 and is known for its excellent acoustics.

The repertoire of the theatre, much like the building itself, has always been heavily influenced by its Italian counterparts. Cimarosa's *La ballerina amante* was the inaugural performance in 1793. Although bowing on occasion to France and Germany, works by Donizetti, Bellini, Rossini and Verdi, to name but a few, have become the standard fare.

Portuguese and Spanish opera have been part of the repertoire since the theatre reopened with Rui Coelho's *Dom João IV* in 1940. A most celebrated production of *La traviata* took place in 1958 with Maria Callas and Alfredo Kraus. More recent performances include Luis de Pablo's Portuguese première of *Kiú* (1987).

The architect: José Da Costa e Silva
The building: Opened 1793
Capacity: About 1100
Opening perfomance: Cimarosa's *La Ballerina Amante*

CARLOTAE
BRASILIAE PRINCIPI
QVOD FELICEM STATVM REI F
REGIA PROLE CONFIRMARIT
THEAT AVSPICATO EXSTR
AVCT DID IGN PIN MANQ P.P.
OLISIPONENSE CIVES
SOLIC AMORE ET LONGA FIDE
ERCA DOMVM AVG PROBATI
IN MON PVBLICAE LAETITIAE
C
ANNO M DCC XCIII.

Jorge Listopad

Located between reality and illusion, the opera house of São Carlos in Lisbon is very beautiful. Nearby, the great Fernando Pessoa (whose father was a music critic) was born on the third floor of a family house whose windows looked out on to the opera. It is a very beautiful theatre indeed, built in the late 18th century, in the Neo-Classical, anti-Baroque style, i.e. modern for its time, and retaining to this day great aesthetic, acoustic and technical qualities, though, like all theatres in the Italian style, it lacks versatility.

For several decades, experimentation and innovation have been key characteristics of the operatic theatre. The lack of adaptability of Italian stages is an obstacle; but do large auditoria have to be synonymous with 'traditional theatre'?

So I searched for an alternative to traditional theatre, albeit inside the São Carlos Opera House. And I chose Salão Nobre, with tall, elegant windows giving on to the terrace over the arcade of the main entrance. The space had been used for receptions, exhibitions and even concerts. I transformed it two or three times, always differently, into a new space, a space for new rituals.

I worked with the stage designers: they took part in the discussions, much in the way that technicians/artists would take part, illuminating and codifying the new concept of the work, the new vision for the costumes, and last but not least, working with actors who sing, of singers who act. Everything gained a new dimension.

I staged a contrapuntal production of a classical Portuguese work *A vingança da cigana,* in which the trees and the natural world appeared to invade the remaining space in the gilded corners. And I saw again a Baroque opera by the famous António José da Silva (burnt alive by the Inquisition) and António Teixeira, *As guerras de Alecrim e Mangerona,* which, by means of a Pirandello-like device, gave each character a marionette double; it had wildly poetic, dreamlike costumes, the coat of mail decorated with flowers and fruit, contrasting with skintight tights enclosing tiny waists.

The opera I seek to create – most recently in an abandoned power plant – knows no boundaries: it needs risk; it wants to be experienced as a great festive occasion; a musical feast, needless to say, but also a feast for the eyes, and for the other senses; an end to winter sleep, awakening the creative intelligence of artists and audience alike. It is an act of restoration, of renewal and much more . . . so much, I could write a book. The operatic theatre was always, and is still, at every performance, something different.

LONDON
ROYAL OPERA HOUSE

Since 1732 there has been a public theatre on the site of the Royal Opera House. The present building dates from 1858 and was the design of E.M. Barry, son of Sir Charles Barry who was architect for the Palace of Westminster, more commonly known as the Houses of Parliament. Barry's Neo-Classical theatre nods to the majestic Greek Revival structure built on the site by Robert Smirke in 1809. Rather plain when compared to most opera houses, there is a bold Corinthian portico of six columns above a rusticated ground floor. The figures of Melpomene and Thalia (Muses of Tragedy and Comedy) by John Flaxman and J.C. Rossi (salvaged from Smirke's theatre) adorn niches on either side of the façade, and the building terminates with double Doric pilasters.

Building technology of the day allowed for construction of the horseshoe-shaped auditorium to be built without obstructions on the upper levels. The interior designer, the Italian Raffaele Monti, used the standard colours of cream, gold and red but included a band of turquoise in the ceiling as a tribute to earlier amphitheatres. The auditorium can accommodate just under 2,200 spectators. In 1899 renovations by the architect Edwin Sachs included the glass enclosure beneath the portico and additional stairways inside.

From the beginning, the theatre was an 'Italian house', and the official name was the Royal Italian Opera House. Virtually all productions, regardless of original score, were performed in Italian. Even Meyerbeer's *Les Huguenots*, sung for the inaugural performance in 1858, was translated into Italian. This practice was ended and the word 'Italian' dropped from the name in 1892 after Gustav Mahler conducted Wagner's *Der Ring des Nibelungen* in German. Today opera is performed in a variety of languages. The Royal Opera House is also the home of the Royal Ballet.

Three years after the 1858 opening, the celebrated soprano Adelina Patti made her Royal Opera House début as Amina in Bellini's *La sonnambula*. This was the beginning of her twenty-four-year reign as diva of the house, a role assumed by Nellie Melba in 1888 until her farewell performance in 1926. Enrico Caruso thrilled audiences for seven seasons between 1902 and 1914.

The Royal Opera House closed in July 1914, and was used for furniture storage during World War I. When it reopened in 1919, various productions from cabaret to films, as well as opera and ballet, used the Royal Opera House. During World War II it served as a dance hall for servicemen, and since it reopened in 1946, with Tchaikovsky's *Sleeping Beauty*, it has been used only for opera and ballet.

In the decade following World War II, many world and British premières were staged – Bliss's *The Olympians* (1949), Vaughan Williams's *The Pilgrim's Progress* (1951), Tippett's *The Midsummer Marriage* (1955), in

addition to Britten's special commission – *Gloriana* – for the coronation of Queen Elizabeth in 1953.

In 1961 Georg Solti proclaimed he would make the Royal Opera House the greatest venue in the world for opera, with productions like *Fidelio* (1961), conducted by Klemperer, and Zeffirelli's *Tosca* (1965) starring Maria Callas, but was not without his critics.

Despite an extension carried out in 1982, lack of reasonable space for dressing and rehearsal rooms, along with poor ventilation prompted an ambitious programme of renovation and expansion. The enlarged and renovated house opened amid much publicity in 1999.

The architects: E.M.Barry, 1858; Jeremy Dixon, 1999
The building: Opened 1858; closed during the wars; enlarged and reopened 1999
Capacity: About 2200
Opening perfomance: Meyerbeer's *Les Huguenots*
World premières: Britten's *Billy Budd*, 1951; Tippett's *The Midsummer Marriage*, 1955
Notable appearances: Joan Sutherland and Maria Callas together in Bellini's *Norma*, 1953

Sir Georg Solti

My first memory of the Royal Opera House, and indeed of England, dates all the way back to 1938. Many British opera lovers believe that I made my Covent Garden début in 1959, but that was only my début there as an *opera* conductor. Twenty-one years earlier I had been engaged as one of the conductors for the Russian Ballet's summer season in London.

The invitation had come about thanks to Antal Doráti, a fellow Hungarian conductor six years my senior, who was at that time Music Director of the Russian Ballet. Central Europe was becoming an increasingly ominous place during the summer of 1938 – the Nazis had taken control of Austria the previous March, on the very day of my conducting début at the Budapest Opera – and it seemed clear that an aspiring twenty-five-year-old conductor who also happened to be Jewish ought to try very hard to find work elsewhere. Doráti had evidently heard good things about me from his father, who played violin in the Budapest Opera orchestra, and he managed to get me a contract.

I stayed at a little bed-and-breakfast in a side-street near the British Museum, but I often had meals at the flat that Doráti, his charming wife and their daughter had taken for the season. I knew no one else in London, spoke only a few words of English and felt too inhibited to use the few words I knew: I remember going to a Lyons Corner House near Covent Garden and pointing to anything at all on the menu, so that I wouldn't have to ask any questions. And of course the weather was awful – rain every day, or so I recall.

I did my studying in the theatre's library, which was in the little building across the street from the main house. It seems to me that rehearsals went well enough, but I can't imagine how I managed to communicate with the players. The ballet master was Michel Fokine, whose name is now legendary; both he and his wife were very friendly towards me. I have few memories of specific performances, but I do remember being unhappy about having to push and pull *tempi* completely out of shape in Schumann's *Carnaval* in order to please the dancers.

I suppose I didn't do too badly, because towards the end of my stay Colonel de Basil, the impresario, called me to his office and offered me a contract to tour Australia with the company. In the end, however, I decided not to sign it; I was sure that I could do better in Europe, and so I returned to the Continent. (The decision nearly cost me my life, but that's another story.) Twenty-three years later, when I became Music Director of the Royal Opera, I was installed in the office in which Colonel de Basil had received me in 1938.

How did my Music Directorship come about? In 1958, Lord Harewood came over to attend one of my performances *(La forza del destino)* at the Frankfurt Opera, where I was General Music Director. He was acting as a sort of talent scout for David Webster, the Royal Opera's General Manager, and he gave a positive report. This is why I was invited to make my début as an opera conductor at the house – a début that took place in December 1959. The work we settled on was *Der Rosenkavalier,* and the cast was extraordinary: Elisabeth Schwarzkopf as the Marschallin, Sena Jurinac as Octavian, Hanny Steffek as Sophie and Kurt Böhme as Ochs. On the basis of those performances, Lord Drogheda, then Chairman of the Royal Opera House, invited me to become Music Director. 'We can't pay much,' he said, 'but you must do it.'

To his surprise, I replied 'After thirteen years as an opera director I want to change my life and do more symphonic work.'

'Don't say no yet. Think it over. We can wait. We haven't got anyone else in mind.'

Not many weeks later, when I was in Los Angeles to work with the Philharmonic, I asked Bruno Walter his advice on the matter. 'You must do it – no question!' he said. 'We, the older generation of opera conductors, are disappearing, and we need not only Karajan but also others among your generation to take our place. If you don't do it, there will be a gap of a generation among opera conductors.' Then he said something I'll never forget: 'The English love talented people, so they will love you. But you will *hate* the climate.'

I thought, 'What a foolish old man! I don't care about the climate – I only want to conduct.' I now know how right he was!

I accepted Lord Drogheda's offer and moved to London. My first full season as Music Director opened in September 1961 with Gluck's *Iphigénie en Tauride.* It was the beginning of one of the most productive decades in my life, and my warm relationship with the house and the company has continued to this day.

London Coliseum

The marriage of Sadler's Wells Opera and its home, the London Coliseum, is a relatively new phenomenon, having taken place in 1968. The 'new' home is the flamboyant edifice opened by theatre manager Oswald Stoll and architect Frank Matcham in St. Martin's Lane on 24 December 1904. Matcham was Britain's most innovative and prolific theatre architect and this is considered to be his finest project. The rusticated façade with projecting balconies and off-centre tower is a familiar sight during the evenings in the West End, when the ball atop the tower is lit (originally it also revolved). Inside can be found alabaster foyers and a sumptuous auditorium with a capacity of almost 2,400. The opera house possessed the first and largest revolving stage of its kind in Britain.

Stoll's intention was to provide a more respectable venue than the popular music hall of the 19th century, a place '. . . where a man could bring his family without fear of shocking them'. Until World War II the opera house played host to a wide variety of performances – from revues such as the *Folies Bergères* and Flo Ziegfeld to Sarah Bernhardt or the Marx Brothers to acrobats and performing animals. In 1909 Stoll invited Sergei Diaghilev to bring his Ballets Russes to the Coliseum and was told by the master: 'The Russian Ballet sandwiched between performing dogs and a fat lady playing a silver-plated trombone? Never! Never!' However, the troupe did perform in 1917.

Under the ownership of Prince Littler (Stoll died in 1942), the Coliseum benefited in the 1940s and 1950s from the popularity of musical theatre. Berlin's *Annie Get Your Gun* ran for three years during this period. Unfortunately the Coliseum found it difficult to compete with other West End theatres and it was leased as a cinema to MGM who chose not to renew the lease in 1967, at the same time as Sadler's Wells Opera realised it had outgrown its Islington premises and was in search of more spacious quarters. Although much had to be done to renovate the building, Sadler's Wells Opera brought a level of prestige long overdue to this important London theatre.

The opera house opened on 21 August 1968 with *Don Giovanni*. English National Opera (renamed from Sadler's Wells Opera in 1974) stages traditional and new works each ten month season, while encouraging both conventional and innovative productions, all sung in English. In a very short period, ENO has developed a superb reputation for one of the most comprehensive and adventurous repertoires to be found, without the elitism that accompanies many houses.

The architect: Frank Matcham
The building: Opened 1904 as a theatre, with the first revolving stage in the UK; 1968 as an opera house
Capacity: About 2400
Opening perfomance: Mozart's *Don Giovanni*
World première: Birtwhistle's *The Mask of Orpheus*, 1986

The Earl of Harewood

When I arrived to work at the Coliseum in 1972, Sadler's Wells Opera (as it still was, though it had left that building nearly four years before) had already embarked on a *Ring* cycle – very successfully too, with *The Valkyrie* some two years before. I knew, because like others I had suffered from it, that the theatre lacked any element of air conditioning so that it was too hot in summer and too draughty in winter, but I had enjoyed what I had heard and seen there before I was asked to work for the company, and prospects were rosy. Actually, prospects usually are: it's realities which can turn a bit grim. Mine didn't, at least not regularly, but that's another story.

Quite early on in my time at this old-fashioned, welcoming theatre, I heard Reginald Goodall talking about the acoustics – Goodall was of course a main (but not the only) reason why the company had decided on a *Ring* cycle. It was quite simple, really. Inside the management of Sadler's Wells there existed a conviction that the greatest Wagnerian conductor in the world was an Englishman who, because his rehearsal methods were painstaking and thorough (another way of saying he was a slow worker and took more rehearsal time than other conductors), was given little opportunity to conduct Wagner (or indeed anything else, but Wagner was what mattered) by his home company at

Covent Garden. So, after a resplendent *Mastersingers* at the pint-sized old theatre at Sadler's Wells and the discovery of a new batch of British Wagnerian singers, we set off on a *Ring* voyage of discovery.

I had heard other conductors at the Coliseum before Goodall, notably Charles Mackerras and Mario Bernardi, and I knew that some people (not me) found the acoustics unreliable, or at least patchy. But Reggie asserted with total conviction that here was an ideal theatre for Wagner, comparable to Bayreuth and much better than what was available elsewhere. Covent Garden was better for Mozart, the Coliseum for Wagner. The reverberation period was greater and the sound therefore warmer and closer to what ideally fitted Wagner's music. That didn't chime with what seemed to come most easily to the singers of the company – operetta as well as Mozart suited the intrinsically lighter voices we had at our disposal – but at least it involved the judgement of an expert, moreover one prepared to put his opinion for some years regularly and splendidly to the test.

I grew to love the building, whatever its lack of basic creature comforts, and the start of a new season – even the start of a new week, after a Sunday of rest – was satisfaction, almost an inspiration. My office was at first backstage, two floors up winding stairs; there was a lift but it was too expensive to put into working order. The fun was to go in each morning through the stage door and past singers and orchestral musicians getting ready for work, and I was disappointed when a recommended redistribution of offices put mine not only into

50

a smaller room but in the front-of-house and therefore less in touch with backstage. If it worked out better, it didn't seem the best plan for the chief executive to cavil over where he camped out; the first day I was in the new office – New Year's Eve – I was telephoning my Chairman before going North for the break, when I looked out of the window which retaliated by falling into the street; not just the window but the frame as well. We were lucky nobody was killed.

Rehearsals were the best part of each week, apart perhaps from a successful first night. There one could see the results of the planning we had done months, even years, before; the designs which had looked good in model tested on the stage; the director's clever notions starting to take shape before being tested on the audience; the young singers promoted one stage in their careers either fulfilling our confidence or, sadly, moving back a step because we had misjudged what they could do. In rehearsal dull moments, even in the umpteenth revival of what had never been a scintillating production, were not what I expected, nor what I often got.

That's what the Coliseum means to me. A theatre full of aspirations, but without ossified traditions; a theatre where you created your own expectations, what you had to live up to. A theatre, therefore, it was a pleasure and an honour to work in.

LYONS
OPÉRA DE LYON

The opera house is not now recognisable from the painting illustrated here, for in 1993, when the Le Nouvel Opéra opened, the architect Jean Nouvel left the façade of the old building with its row of Muses and arches but added a semicircular glazed structure, doubling the height of the original building. Some mixtures of styles work well, like the pyramids at the Louvre, but this addition is perhaps a little too robust, so it is good to see the opera house before Jean Nouvel got to it.

Opera in Lyons was first performed at the Académie Royale de Musique in 1687 and continued to provide entertainment several times a week until the inevitable fire destroyed the building in 1688. It was not until 1756 that a new theatre for *opéra comique* and *opera buffa* was established. The Grand Théâtre, which is the original building upon which the recent restoration has been carried out, was built by Chenavard and Pollet in 1831 and enlarged in 1837. The repertoire included works by Wagner, Verdi, Bellini, Donizetti and French composers Massenet and Gounod – the popular sentimental operas the people were so fond of at the time.

From 1955 to 1970 the Opéra de Lyon was administered by Paul Camerlo, followed by his nephew Louis Erlo who brought the house up-to-date with an adventurous production policy. The English musical director John Eliot Gardiner, appointed in 1986, changed the repertoire towards classical and Baroque operas. Kent Nagano took over in 1988 to see through the rebuilding. In the new theatre his success is monitored by a system of lights that illuminate the exterior of the building – the more people in the audience the brighter the house glows.

The architects: Antoine-Marie Chenavard and Jean-Marie Pollet, 1831; Jean Nouvel, 1993
The building: Opened 1831; extended with revolutionary roof 1993
Capacity: About 1100
Opening perfomance: Boieldieu's *La Dame Blanche*
World première: Schönberg's *Erwartung*, 1967

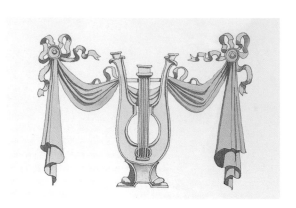

MADRID
TEATRO LÍRICO NACIONAL
LA ZARZUELA

In the 17th century, opera in Spain was reserved solely for the pleasure of royalty. As early as 1629, the court of Philip IV staged Lope de Vega's *La selva sin amor*. The tradition of royal patronage continued in the 18th century under Philip V. In 1737, after the famed Italian castrato Farinelli performed in Madrid, Philip appointed him to sing the same four songs every night as a remedy for melancholia. Farinelli did this for over twenty years until 1759 when he was sent into exile by Charles II, a ruler who found Italian opera undignified.

With roots as early as 1660 in *La purpura de la rosa* (music by Hidalgo, libretto by Calderón de la Barca), the 'zarzuela' was born. This light form of comic opera, often with spoken dialogue, took its name from the brambles (*zarzas*) found outside the Zarzuela Palace where King Juan Carlos lives today. Given the negative attitude towards Italian opera shown by Charles II, the zarzuela was able to emerge as a national form of Spanish opera after more

than a century of Italian domination. The interest in this style continued and on 10 October 1856 the Teatro Lírico Nacional La Zarzuela opened. Designed by architect Jeronimó de la Gándara, the theatre became the principal venue of zarzuela in Spain.

The design of the interior and exterior were heavily influenced by Italian opera houses. The somewhat small horseshoe-shaped auditorium now seats just over 1,200 people. In 1866 José Maria Guallart altered various parts of the theatre, installing a grand Neo-Renaissance staircase and changing much of the interior decoration. The theatre burned down in 1909 and was rebuilt with a metal super-

structure by Cesare Iradier in 1913.

By 1955 the theatre had deteriorated to the extent that it was scheduled for demolition, but thanks to the Society of Spanish Writers, architects Vallejo and Dempierre renovated and restored the theatre in time for the reopening, held on the hundredth anniversary of its inauguration with a performance of *Doña Francisquita* by Amadeo Vives.

For many years the Teatro La Zarzuela has hosted both the native operatic form as well as traditional Italian opera. It has also been a popular venue for Spain's leading contemporary composers. Of particular note, La Zarzuela hosted the premières of Luis de Pablo's *Kiú* (1983) and *El viajero indiscreto* (1990). In 1992 it was also the venue for the much acclaimed opera *The Duenna* by Roberto Gerhard.

The architect: Jeronimó de la Gándara
The building: Opened 1856; home of Spanish comic opera - *La Zarzuela*
Capacity: About 1200
World premières: Pablo's *Kiú*, 1983, and *El viajero indiscreto*, 1990

Julio Bravo

In the bosom of old Madrid, lying by the side of Congress, hidden on Jovellanos Street by two grey blocks of flats and offices, nestles the Teatro La Zarzuela. This beautiful Neo-Classical edifice, built in scarcely seven months by Jeronimó de la Gándara in 1856, has fulfilled for the last thirty years – with modesty and enthusiasm – the role of Madrid's opera house.

The Zarzuela was built with the help of a capitalist benefactor, Francisco de la Riva, at a time when theatrical Madrid was booming. Only six years earlier the Teatro Real had opened its doors, to be followed in the years after by the Teatro Circo, the Talía, the Variedades, the Novedades, the Príncipe Alfonso and the Rossini.

The birth of the Teatro La Zarzuela coincided with the most fertile period of zarzuela, the Spanish musical genre *par excellence*.

The genre sprouted at the beginning of the 17th century, but did not reach maturity until the arrival of composers like Barbieri, Arrieta or Gaztambide, the predecessors of the greats – Bretón, Chapí, Chueca, Giménez and Vives – who gave zarzuela its golden

age between 1875 and 1925. The decline of the genre in the first quarter of the 20th century prompted the decline and closure of the Teatro too.

It reopened in 1956, its centenary, with the staging of *Doña Francisquita*. A young tenor, Alfredo Kraus, made his début on the occasion, later rising to legendary status. The revitalisation of the Teatro had begun, and was generally thought to have culminated eight years later with a staging of *Tosca*.

But for many years after that, stricken by a shortage of money, the Teatro could 'stage' only voices, although a variety of opera's great names – both Spanish and foreign – sang there. Few will forget the Teatro's production in 1970 of *La bohème*, sung by Mirella Freni and Luciano Pavarotti, regarded by *madrileños* as the finest event since the theatre's foundation.

Yet the Teatro La Zarzuela is a place of small-scale beauty and difficult acoustics; the stage is no wider that 12 metres at its mouth, the seating capacity only 1,200. The hope lives on, which I share with not just a few, that the theatre will return to its origins one day, and become again the home of zarzuela, a genre to which it is so well suited.

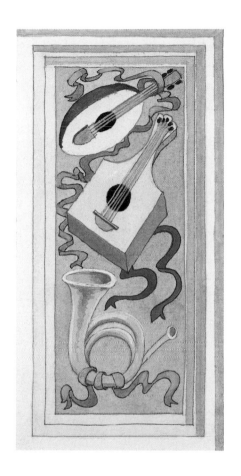

MADRID
TEATRO REAL

While Madrid's Teatro Lírico Nacional La Zarzuela is the home of the national form of Spanish opera, the Teatro Real was the home of Italian opera from the 1850s until a gradual decline in this form of opera and structural problems with the building itself forced closure in 1925. The theatre reopened in 1966 for use as a concert hall only, and the ambitious reconstruction programme which started in 1988, and completed in 1998, has created a 'new' venue for truly world-class opera.

Tunku Varadarajan

When Carmen Alborch, the minister for culture in Spain's former socialist government, visited the scaffolding-ridden Teatro Real in November 1995, a 2½ tonne chandelier hurtled down from the ornate ceiling, killing no one. It could, of course, have flattened her flat, as Falstaff might have put it.

'So near, yet so far,' a wag muttered at the time, summing up in five words of cynicism the history of Madrid's opera house. Opened in 1850, the Teatro had known only seventy-five years of opera, the last performance before the opening of 1998 being an exhilarating *La bohéme* – so the history books say – on 4 November 1925.

The theatre may have made its début with Donizetti's *La favorita*, but the place has had enough ill-luck to earn for itself the sobriquet *el maldito*, or the accursed one. Closed ('for repairs') between 1925 and 1966, it was reopened by General Franco as a concert hall, only to close once more on 14 October 1988. Until 1998, there had been no music, only silence.

Yet Madrid is a place where rumours stalk the streets, and one rumour had it that opera would return to the Teatro Real in 1998. This rumour was the worthy successor of the others that had also told of a reopening, in 1990, in 1992, and again in 1995. If rumours were worth their weight in music, Madrid would have been Europe's opera capital. Instead, like Spain itself, it was an operatically barren place, crying out for musical drama of quality, the one missing ingredient that withheld true metropolitan greatness from Madrid.

Opera's absence for so long is puzzling, especially as Spain has produced a galaxy of modern stars. The late Pilar Lorengar, Montserrat Caballé, Plácido Domingo, Alfredo Kraus, Teresa Berganza, José Carreras. And to think that more operas have been set in Spain than in any other country.

But the better acquainted I became with Madrid, the more convinced I was that *madrileños*, a perverse tribe if ever there was one, were secretly pleased by their city's operatic infamy. The wreck of the Real allowed them to fulminate. The prolonged silences permitted them to rant. 'Damned philistine Franco!'/'Damned politicians!'/'Wretched socialists!'/'Wretched conservatives!'

'Will the repairs to the Teatro Real ever finish?' asked an exasperated headline in *ABC*, the monarchist Madrid daily, in 1957. 'The repairs to the Teatro Real will cost three times

more than had been anticipated,' read another headline, this time in *El País*, in 1992, thirty-five years later. Yet while worthy leader-writers raged against the endless *culebrón*, or soap opera, of the opera house, there were others who quietly adopted the Teatro Real as an amiable mascot-in-stone of lovable, inept, unchanging Spain.

The responsible lady-minister of culture, as feisty as her predecessors, has made frequent visits to the opera house. No chandeliers have so far fallen on her head, but the Teatro Real now has a full season of programming.

The building: Opened 1850; closed 1925 due to structural problems, reopened 1998
Capacity: About 1600
Opening perfomances: Donizetti's *La favorita*, 1850; Falla's *The Three-Cornered Hat*, 1998

MARSEILLES
OPÉRA MUNICIPAL

O pera has been enjoyed in Marseilles since the 16th century. Even in the Roman period of the 2nd century BC, a theatre was built for musical and theatrical productions. The style of the present opera house, the Opéra Municipal, is the result of two distinct periods of architecture. Originally designed by Bernard in the Neo-Classical period of the late 18th century, the opera opened in 1787 by royal permission with Champein's *La mélomanie*. Throughout the 19th century the repertoire was dominated by the works of Halévy and Meyerbeer.

An electrical fire in 1919, following a rehearsal for *L'Africaine*, completely destroyed the auditorium and backstage areas. The team of architects Ebrard, Castel et Raymond retained the original walls and portico whilst installing a lavish Art Deco interior of gold and marble. Deco details were also integrated into the scheme of the enlarged façade. Bas-reliefs at the attic storey of the façade and frescoes throughout the reception areas and auditorium are by important artists of the early 20th century. With its original peristyle still intact, it is a curious yet successful mix of Neo-Classical and Art Deco design, and the imaginative and innovative style contrasts sharply with the grand opera houses of the late 19th century.

The new reinforced concrete building not only reduces the risk of fire but also means there are fewer obstructions for the spectator. The circular auditorium has crimson upholstery on carved mahogany seats; a multitude of silver ornamentation on the walls is set against a background of multi-coloured Portuguese marble. The handful of boxes adjacent to the stage are angled slightly towards the audience in true Italian fashion. The capacity of the opera house is just under two thousand, a quarter of which is for tickets in the 'gods'. The Marseilles audience has developed a preference for the opportunity to interact closely as a part of the total social experience, and this preference probably accounts for the ritual of queuing in the street for tickets before a performance.

The season of the Opéra Municipal runs from October to May and includes ballets

and concerts and there is a loyal roster of artists with international reputations who perform regularly: Martine Dupuy, a native daughter; Leonie Rysanek returns annually; Leo Nucci has never forgotten his early successes here before going out to the world.

In 1984 the Opéra Municipal was the venue for the French première of Milhaud's *Christophe Colomb*. In 1992/3 its production of Richard Strauss's *Die Frau ohne Schatten* won the prize 'Meilleur Spectacle Musical en Région'.

The architects: Bérnard and Ebrard, 1787; Casteland Raymond, 1924
The building: Opened 1787; fire 1919, reopened 1924
Capacity: About 1800
Opening perfomances: Champein's *Mélomanie*, 1787; Reyer's *Sigurd*, 1924

MILAN
TEATRO ALLA SCALA

In the history of opera, no other house has been so highly revered, so often imitated, nor so regularly used as a standard for comparison as La Scala. But La Scala, as it is usually called, is much more than a beautiful place for opera, it symbolises the essence of character and pride of local culture typical of the Milanese. For this reason more than any other, the reopening of the opera house in 1946 after the bad damage caused by Allied bombs in 1943 was the most promising sign that the oppression of Mussolini's regime and the horrors of World War II were finally over.

After the fire in 1776 that destroyed the Teatro Regio Ducale of 1717, architect Giuseppe Piermarini was appointed to design a new theatre. Maria-Theresa, Empress of Austria and Duchess of Milan, also an opera enthusiast, gave permission for the new theatre to be built on the site of the church of Santa Maria della Scala. The building was inaugurated in 1778 with a performance of Salieri's *Europa riconosciuta* (the commission having been declined by Gluck). The exterior was planned to be rather simple in design with a rusticated ground floor. The façade gradually breaks forward with a series of bays framed by pairs of pilasters or engaged columns. The original three-bay carriage entrance is topped by a triangular pediment.

The full effect of the theatre was reserved for the interior. The red, gold and white boxes are reached by a maze of reception rooms, stairways and corridors. Massive fluted columns frame the stage with their capitals, stop fluting and bases picked out in gold. The horseshoe-shaped auditorium is vast, with a seating capacity of 2,200 made up of 678 stalls, two galleries and four tiers of boxes. It throbs inside – a reflection of its history, its traditions, its memories and, especially, its twittering and unruly audience.

La Scala and its restless audience has a mind and will of its own, which just like any orchestra, director or performer, can make or break a production. This is especially true of opening night, which is always 7 December, the feast of Milan's patron, St. Ambrose, when the crowd is even more impatient and demanding than usual. Opening night is the society event of the season.

Volumes are written on the people and events which have shaped La Scala's incomparable 220-year history. In 1904, the première of Puccini's *Madama Butterfly* did so badly that it was quietly removed from the programme until 1925. A moving tale centres on Arturo Toscanini who conducted the première of *Turandot* in 1926. Puccini had died and the opera was completed by Franco Alfano. When he reached the part where Puccini stopped composing, Toscanini put down his baton, turned to the audience and said, 'Here the opera ends, because at this point the maestro died', and left the podium. Toscanini was associated with La Scala during various periods from his appointment as Artistic Director in 1898 until

1929 when artistic, financial and political problems in the face of the growing Fascist movement prompted his resignation.

Since its beginnings, La Scala has been a significant artistic and political institution. For a time it was the only location in Milan where gambling was permitted, the profits from this helping to finance performances. In the early 19th century the theatre began the practice of hosting each year the première of an important opera – in some years it may even be two or three – and in so doing La Scala has acquired an international reputation beneficial for the theatre itself, the artists, and the greater acceptance of the operas themselves.

The architect: Giuseppe Piermarini
The building: Opened 1778; bomb damage 1943, reopened 1946
Capacity: About 2200
Opening perfomance: Salieri's *Europa riconosciuta*
World premières: Verdi's *Un Giorno di Regno*, 1840; *Nabucco*, 1842

Vincenzo La Scola

I have a special relationship with La Scala, since my début there was as Pavarotti's substitute in the lead role of *L'elisir d'amore*, on the first night of the production directed by Giuseppe Patané, in 1988. Only four days before the show was meant to go on, Pavarotti had been 'taken ill'. I was Pavarotti's understudy. And when I went on, I was terrified. I was well prepared, of course, but it was a very controversial production. During the performance people in the audience whistled and booed – and not only from the *loggione* – to the point that they interrupted the performance. It wasn't at me that they were booing, but at the direction. At the end of the performance, I was applauded for a full five minutes.

It was my trial by fire: either now or never, I thought. And on I went. At first, my voice was a bit cold, but I soon warmed up. It was an *opera buffa*, you see, and one that I really thoroughly enjoyed, and so eventually I got into it. It was very good for me, and a great way to début at a theatre.

What has always struck me most about La Scala is its sense of the past, and its ceiling. When you enter this opera house, where the ushers wear livery, you are entering not only a theatre, but also history. You see Maestro Riccardo Muti on the podium, but as you soak in the sense of the past from the surroundings, and the pictures on the walls, you suddenly wonder if you are not about to see Toscanini conducting instead.

La Scala is the most complex theatre in the world, not only because it has played host to countless performances, but because the history of opera was played out there, in the sense that so many operas were written for La Scala, and had their first nights there. The same could be said for La Fenice in Venice, but not – although it, too, is a great opera house – the Met in New York.

Then there is the ceiling. During rehearsals, I often stare at that ceiling for periods of fifteen minutes at a time. Usually the ceilings of opera houses are heavily decorated, like churches. La Scala's is stark white with white plasterwork decoration. The reason why I look so long at the ceiling is to do as Caruso did, although please don't think I consider myself to be on his level. He said he used to try to stare at the highest point in a theatre, and to try to throw his voice there. Taking a page from his book, I began to sing looking upwards, and so I would see the lights or the ceiling. Often, in fact, the point that I fix on in a theatre is the exit light. But if not, I like to look at the ceiling.

This vast expanse of nothingness made me feel even more vulnerable on my first night. Faced with the great spread of the stalls, this completely white ceiling makes me feel naked. It's as though there were nothing between the stalls and the sky. At Covent Garden, by contrast, I feel protected. And in La Scala, who wouldn't want to feel protected?

Monaco
Opéra de Monte Carlo

Thanks to the far-sighted outlook of Prince Charles III in the 1850s, the Principality of Monaco has capitalised on its position in the world, geographically and financially, to create a unique niche as the most important resort for the rich and famous. Prince Charles took advantage of the growth of the railway, the lack of legalised gambling in France and Italy and a beautiful climate to establish a resort superior to those found in Germany and Belgium. Likewise, the splendid opera house designed by Charles Garnier, who had recently finished the Paris Opéra, reflects the fairy-tale reputation Monaco has come to enjoy. The theatre stands on the edge of the Mediterranean, joined to the Casino with a foyer of red marble columns. Garnier was commissioned in 1878 to replace the concert hall which had been built on the site only six years before. After less than six months and the efforts of more than four hundred Italian craftsmen, the result was a lavish Second Empire façade with excessively ornamented towers and sculpture by Gustave Doré and Sarah Bernhardt.

Inside, the opulent auditorium exceeds, if possible, the exterior in the use of gilding, carving and applied plaster work. Obviously the Prince's Box is the focal point, seemingly suspended below a cushion canopy of carved swags and drapery. (This was added during the reign of Albert I just after the turn of the 20th century when the seating configuration was altered from the original.) Individual gilded chairs in the stalls complete the relatively small space that accommodates less than six hundred spectators.

The Salle Garnier opened on 25 January 1879 with a spectacle that included ballet, music, opera and a reading by Sarah Bernhardt. This established the

tradition that the theatre would be used for all forms of stage productions. The first opera, Planquette's *Le chevalier Gaston,* was held two weeks later. In the 1880s the opera gained world-class status through the combined efforts of the American opera-lover Alice Heine,

The architect: Charles Garnier
The building: Opened 1879
Capacity: About 500
Opening opera: Planquette's *Le chevalier Gaston*
World premières: Puccini's *La rondine,* 1917; Ravel's *L'enfant et les sortilèges,* 1925

wife of Albert I, and the appointment of the flamboyant Raoul Gunsbourg as director. The favourite singer of Princess Alice was the famed tenor Francesco Tamagno and she was instrumental in making him the Salle Garnier's leading attraction after he sang the title role in Verdi's *Otello* in 1894. In 1899 he created the role of Hélion in De Lara's *Messaline*.

Between 1879 and 1996 there were no less than eighty world premières, among them Puccini's *La rondine* (1917) and Ravel's *L'enfant et les sortilèges* (1925). Two premières by César Franck were held posthumously. *Hulda* (1894) and *Ghisèle* (1896). Critics and audiences were unanimous in their praise for the 1902 season when Nellie Melba and Enrico Caruso performed Puccini's *La bohème* and Verdi's *Rigoletto*. Two years later, Melba sang the title role in the première of Saint-Saëns' *Hélène*. The same composer saw the world première of his *Déjanire* at the Salle Garnier in 1910.

In 1902 Massenet began a decade-long association with the première of *Le jongleur de Notre Dame*, which was followed by performances of his *Chérubin* (1905), *Thérèse* (1907) and *Don Quichotte* (1910). Gunsbourg exceeded his own outstanding record in 1909 when he managed to stage not only Wagner's entire *Der Ring des Nibelungen* but also fourteen additional operas. Diaghilev's Ballets Russes performed *Le spectre de la rose* at the Salle Garnier in 1911 with designs by Pablo Picasso. The company returned 'in exile' to their adopted base after World War I.

MONTPELLIER
OPÉRA MONTPELLIER

The original theatre for Montpellier was designed in 1755 by Jean-Philippe Mareschal, engineer to the crown and director of public works for the province. This was of a rather simple design and based on a French U-shaped plan (as opposed to the more common Italian horseshoe-shaped plan). The theatre burned down for the first time in 1785 and was reconstructed in 1787. The mid-19th century saw many improvements with the addition of numerous paintings by Jean Beaudoin and the installation of a gas chandelier; but the theatre burned down again in April 1881.

A group of judges, including Charles Garnier, best known as architect of the Paris Opéra and the Opéra de Monte Carlo, selected a new design by anonymous entrants. Surprisingly, the competition was won by the two-times Prix de Rome winner Marie-Joseph Cassien-Bernard who had served since 1876 as the Inspector of Works for Garnier's Opéra in Paris.

Montpellier is a Huguenot capital and it was most important that the design be appropriately restrained. As Cassien-Bernard's second Prix de Rome project was a Protestant temple, he was obviously well prepared for this task. A modified rusticated base gives way to treble arches with giant-order Corinthian columns, while a recessed attic storey rests behind a balustrade. The allegorical grouping around the clock is by Antonin Injalbert who also designed sculptural details for the Hôtel de Ville in Paris. Cassien-Bernard was inspired by the work of his fellow classmate Gaspard André at the Théâtre des Célestins in Lyons. Inside, the auditorium is reached by various stairways and anterooms similarly styled. Virtually all interior ornament and painting, also appropriately restrained for Huguenot tastes, were done by regional artists such as Ernest Michel from Montpellier,

Arnaud Durbecq from Marseilles and Auguste Baussan from Avignon.

Despite constant tensions between architect and city, as is so often the case, the Opéra opened on schedule: 1 October 1888. The first performance was, of course, *Les Huguenots* by Meyerbeer.

The architect: Marie-Joseph Cassien-Bernard
The building: Opened 1888
Capacity: About 1500
Opening perfomance: Meyerbeer's *Les Huguenots*

Moscow
Bolshoi Theatre

The original theatre on this site, the Grand Petrovsky Theatre, was completed by Osip Bovet and Andrei Mikhailov in 1824. Bovet was probably the most prominent architect in Moscow at the time. Prior to building the Grand (Bolshoi) Theatre, he was the principal architect for the Kremlin as well as being responsible for the rebuilding of Moscow after the fire during the war against Napoleon of 1812. When the theatre burned down in 1853, only the portico and walls remained. In 1856 it was rebuilt as we know it today by Alberto Cavos, who was also the architect of the Maryinsky (Kirov) Theatre in St. Petersburg.

Proportionally the building appears very heavy. This is exaggerated by the use of rusticated stone through all floors and an eight-column portico of composite columns. Atop the portico stands a chariot with Apollo, god of the arts, drawn by four exuberant steeds. The bronze group tends to pull the eye upwards and gives the façade much more movement than it otherwise would have.

Inside Cavos installed a very opulent, rather large Italian-style auditorium that seats in excess of 2,100. Five loge levels and a gallery, all faced in gold and each set back a little further than the one below, rise towards a ceiling decoration in cream and gold. An Imperial Box stands prominently in the centre and all is upholstered in red.

Throughout the 19th century, particularly during the reign of Alexander I, productions in Russia encompassed a wide variety, from German to French to Italian works in addition to native opera. By the end of the century, works by Tchaikovsky appeared frequently along with other favourite sons such as Mussorgsky and Rimsky-Korsakov. It was also the time when the ballet master Aleksandr Gorsky was training dancers in the style still emulated today. After the 1917 Revolution the theatre came to dominate the Soviet cultural landscape. Many notable Soviet operas had their premières at the Bolshoi including Shaporin's *The Decembrists* in 1953 and Prokofiev's *War and Peace* in 1959.

Although the Bolshoi is one of the most famous theatres in the world, setting high standards for both opera and ballet, it has also been the 'scene' of many important social and political events, particularly during the Soviet era. It played host to various meetings

of the All-Russia Congress of Soviets where Lenin spoke regularly during the early years after the 1917 Revolution. In 1921 it was the venue for the proclamation calling for the formation of the Union of Soviet Socialist Republics. In World War II, the Bolshoi was damaged in October 1941 during an air raid but was completely restored before the end of the war.

The architect: Alberto Cavos
The building: Opened 1856; bomb damage 1941, restored by 1942
Capacity: About 2100
Opening perfomance: Bellini's *I Puritani*
World première: Prokofiev's *War and Peace*, 1959

Galina Vishnevskaya

A production of *Eugene Onegin* was in preparation under the direction of Boris Pokrovsky . . . and I was allowed to rehearse with him [as Tatyana]. It was the first time I had worked with this man, who was to change all my notions of operatic theatre. (Later, I created all my roles with him.) From the very first, he became for me an absolute authority, a repository from which I could draw all the secrets of the art of opera. If I had not met him, I surely would have left the Bolshoi.

I underwent such inner conflict over the role of Tatyana that I almost came to hate it. I came to the rehearsal not only without any desire to work but with a firm resolve to refuse the part. But I couldn't imagine arguing with Pokrovsky, since I hadn't yet demonstrated my artistic worth.

'Sit at the desk, take a sheet of paper, a quill pen, and sing.'

I began: 'Let me perish . . .'

How many Tatyanas had already been heard in the theatre! The Bolshoi had seven at that time.

I sang, and with every facial expression I could muster I tried to show him how boring and uninteresting it was: This scene is insufferably long – let it be over soon!

I sang the whole scene through. He said nothing, and I didn't care. Here it comes – I thought, he'll say that it was bad, that I'm not suited for the role. Fine. Maybe I'll get Aïda.

Finally he began, 'I watch you, and I'm amazed. Such a young girl, and she whines like a little old woman suffering from rheumatism. How can you sing Tatyana like that?'

'Of course one shouldn't sing Tatyana like that, but I don't like the part. I find it boring.'

He shouted, 'You don't like the part? You find it bor-r-ring? Why do you sit there like

an old woman on a feather bed? You have to understand that Tatyana is seventeen. You have to understand what kind of novels she has devoured, and the state that she – a well-bred young lady – must have been in to make a declaration of love out of the blue and write it in a letter to a young man. And you're bored! All you sopranos want to play African and Ethiopian princesses, anything the audience doesn't understand. Just try to play Pushkin's Tatyana and see how far you get! Did you read what Tchaikovsky wrote? "Rapturously! Passionately!" But you singers are all fools. You don't even know how to read. Did you read this? Did you understand it?'

I jumped to my feet and shouted back, 'What do you mean, "understand"? I look at the stage and see nothing of what you describe. But you staged this production, and so it

must suit you, it must be what you want!'

'Don't look at the stage. Learn to use your own brains. "Rapturously! Passionately!" She shouldn't get out of bed as if she were being hoisted by a crane. She should fly! Have you ever been sledding?'

'Of course.' I saw that his eyes were shining, that he was shouting and on fire.

'Well, if you've been sledding, that's what Tatyana's letter is all about. Without thinking, she got on a sled and, from a high, steep hill, flew down! It took her breath away. It wasn't until she reached the bottom, until the sled stopped, that she came to her senses. In the same way, Tatyana wrote the letter and sent it to Onegin. Only later did she realise what she had done.'

I was listening, mouth agape, unaware that tears had long been streaming from my eyes. Suddenly, as if by magic, I saw myself as I was in Kronstadt – Galka the Artistka, writing her first love letter to the boy with the parting in his hair. My heart began to ache sweetly, to flutter in my breast, and the radiant, sweet image of Tatyana, the Tatyana of my childhood in all her unique charm, appeared before me.

From the very first, that remarkable director and psychologist took into account my individuality, and my young, resonant voice. With his keen insight into personalities, he had sensed my impulsiveness, my temper. That day, without my even suspecting it, he gave me the key to 'my theatre' – a key I had long carried within me. And from then on, I threw myself headlong into work – into shattering those traditional conventions that had seemed as indestructible as the world.

Without looking back, and as one emancipated, I entered the struggle, defending my own art. Had I been an inexperienced novice, the Bolshoi would have soon broken me, relegating me to the ranks of ordinary, good singers. I would not have become an individual personality and certainly never could have created a new operatic style at the Bolshoi.

MUNICH
BAYERISCHE STAATSOPER

The opera house has long been a favourite form of corporate boasting. Munich has been no slouch here, albeit with some justification: oldest orchestra and choir in Germany (1523), first free-standing (as opposed to part of palace) opera house (1654) in Germany, and today, just pipped to the post by the Bastille, the second largest opera stage in the world – 2,452 square metres.

The first opera house in Munich, a converted corn exchange, was built by the Elector Ferdinand Maria. This helped to forge that link between court and bourgeoisie at a cultural level that has always proved fruitful. For the next hundred years, however, opera still served mainly a politically correct and highly decorative function of praising rulers and the *status quo,* albeit in the Italian language, using Italian composers, musicians and singers. To further this trend, in 1753 a new theatre was built in the Residenz (the palace) by the French architect François Cuvilliés. It is still standing today, now called after its architect, and is used for smaller-scale opera productions.

But by the last decades of the 18th century, the wind of the Enlightenment and revolution were creating waves in Munich, and the old themes of court opera were giving way to sometimes rather cosy stories from daily life, often written by German composers and sung in German, and aimed at the bourgeoisie, not the court. By the end of the century, music was firmly woven into the fabric of the city, and then as now was often the subject of impassioned argument. A prohibition on Italian opera imposed in

1787 was lifted in 1805, but German opera continued to be vigorously promoted; Weber's *Abu Hassan* was premièred in 1811 and his *Der Freischütz* reached Munich in 1822.

In 1811 Maximilian I laid the foundation stone of what we now know as the Nationaltheater on the Max-Joseph Platz, and there, on 12 October 1818, after many political and financial upheavals, the young architect Carl von Fischer's opera house finally opened, with Ferdinand Fränzl's *Singspiel, Die Weihe.* This building burned down in January 1823; the extinguisher system, very advanced for its time, failed to work because the water supply, in tanks on the roof, was frozen solid. The house was rebuilt in two years, financed by a one pfennig tax on beer – an apt and easy way to raise money in Bavaria. The building, with its eight Corinthian columns and generally massive appearance, must have seemed a bit over-the-top in a city of 54,000 inhabitants. With seats for two thousand in stalls and five circles, rising vertically in the Italian manner, it was – and is – an imposing sight, inside and out.

In 1825, with the accession of Ludwig I and the reopening of the opera house,

a period began of musical activity in this small town (even today with a population of just over one million) rivalled only by Vienna. One strength of musical life in Munich has always been an ability to hire effective movers and shakers, and the appointment in 1836

The architect: Carl von Fischer
The building: Opened 1818; fire 1823, reconstructed 1825; bomb damage 1943, reopened 1963
Capacity: About 2100
Opening perfomance: Fränzl's *Singspiel Die Weihe*
World premières: Wagner's *Tristan und Isolde* 1865; *Die Meistersinger von Nürnberg* 1868; *Das Rheingold* 1869; *Die Walküre* 1870

of the composer Franz Lachner as *Hofkapellmeister*, then *Generalmusikdirektor*, was particularly fortunate. During his thirty-year tenure, he brought the operas of Meyerbeer, Verdi, Donizetti, Auber, Halévy, Gounod and many more to the Nationaltheater, not to mention his own operas (fair enough), three of which were performed there.

The great turning point came in 1864, with the accession of the nineteen-year-old Ludwig II, who immediately called Richard Wagner to Munich. *Tannhäuser* and *Lohengrin* had already been heard in Munich, conducted by Lachner, but with Wagner's arrival and the dramatic growth of the Wagner cult, Lachner drew back and finally threw in the sponge in 1868, leaving an instrumental and vocal ensemble capable of the enormous demands Wagner made on it. The new *Hofkappellmeister* Hans von Bülow conducted the premières of Wagner's next two operas, *Tristan und Isolde* and *Die Meistersinger* there, but left Munich in 1869 when his wife Cosima deserted him for Wagner. Then in 1869 and 1870 followed *Das Rheingold* and *Die Walküre*.

In October 1943 the Nationaltheater was reduced to rubble. Opera resumed in November 1945 in the Prinzregententheater. This remained Munich's main opera house until 1963, when the Nationaltheater, rebuilt to Carl von Fischer's original design, reopened.

Not everything has gone smoothly since the meticulous reconstruction: the opera house was closed down from 1987 to 1989 for renewal of all the stage machinery, then disaster struck in 1992 when bacteria were discovered in the oil lubricating the rollers along which huge sections of stage equipment moved, making their movements erratic and unreliable, and therefore highly dangerous. The whole house was once again closed for almost a year, reopening in autumn 1993.

Under a distinguished succession of top names, from Sir Georg Solti from 1946 to 1952, to Peter Jonas today, the Bavarian State Opera has continued its tradition of core repertoire as well as new work, some specially commissioned, for instance the young Hans-Jürgen von Bose's *Schlachthof 5* (Slaughterhouse 5), premièred in July 1996.

NEW YORK
METROPOLITAN OPERA HOUSE

The Metropolitan Opera House is part of the Lincoln Center complex dedicated to the performing arts. The three buildings surround the rectangular plaza which is elevated above and open to Columbus Avenue. The buildings with flat roofs and colonnades are covered in white marble and arranged in a classical austere layout and style.

The approach, up a long low set of steps from Columbus Avenue, leads directly ahead to the Metropolitan Opera House which was built in 1966 to the design of the architect Wallace K. Harrison. On the left is the New York State Theater, built in 1964; on the right is the Avery Fisher Hall, built in 1962.

Behind the impressive tall arches of the Metropolitan Opera House is the sumptuous lobby which is dominated by two large and splendid murals by Marc Chagall.

The whole complex is best appreciated at night when the buildings and fountain are illuminated.

The architect: Wallace Harrison
The building: Opened 1966
Capacity: About 3800
Opening perfomance: Barber's *Anthony and Cleopatra*
World première: Glass's *The Voyage* 1992

Paul Gruber

In its 116-year history, the Metropolitan Opera has had two homes. When in 1966 the company moved from its original theatre on Broadway and 39th Street to its new one at Lincoln Center, the common way to differentiate between the two was 'Old Met' and 'New Met'. Now, thirty-four years later, it seems odd to talk about a 'New Met'. No building can stay new forever.

The Old Met was demolished in January 1967, a few months after the company's first performances in its new home. I am a lover of old theatres, and after all these years I am still sorry that I never had a chance to see this one, much less to hear a performance in it. In my work, I've spent many hours pouring over photographs of its interior and exterior, and feel I know it is as well as one can know a building one has never set foot in. No photograph taken after the 19th century makes the exterior look attractive and most of the theatre's lobby areas look disappointingly drab, but one can understand why the Old Met's auditorium was long considered one of the glories of New York.

The auditorium of the Met's current home is likewise its most successful feature. The entire building may be permanently stuck in 1966 – not an era most of us would like to be suspended in – but the interior seems to have aged better than the façade. I like it best when I show it to people who have never seen it before: the Austrian crystal chandeliers still have the ability to inspire wonder – whether they're standing still or ascending, as they do before each performance – and the red-and-gold colour scheme, brought over from the old house gives the auditorium a warmth that the rest of the building lacks. Depending on where one sits, the theatre's size and shape can make the stage and everything that takes place on it seem incidental to the rest of the room; on the other hand, I've been to enough great performances there to know that the right singers can make this 3,800-seat house seem like a salon.

After a while, old theatres develop a wonderful smell, a rich, musty odour of absorbed laughter, tears and wonderment. There have been plenty of all three at the Lincoln Center Met, but it has yet to have earned its smell.

Paris
Palais Garnier

The long and venerable history of the opera in Paris reached something of a milestone when the Opéra, properly known as the Théâtre National de l'Opéra, took up residence in the Palais Garnier on 5 January 1875; from that moment, until opera performances ceased in 1987 prior to the opening of the Opéra Bastille, the Paris Opéra meant Garnier's glorious cathedral to opera at the busy junction of the boulevard des Capucines, the rue de la Chaussée-d'Antin and the rue Neuve-des-Maturins.

The site was identified in a decree of September 1860, and the architectural competition unveiled, with a frighteningly tight one-month deadline for entries, the following December. The winner, Charles Garnier, was announced on 29 May 1861, and the early months of construction were marked by continuous pumping to drain the swampy site of water; in the intervening years before opera began at the theatre, Garnier saw his huge, labyrinthine (and remarkably dry) edifice being used as a food store during the Paris Commune of 1869-70. Parisians rapidly took the Palais Garnier to their hearts, and no wonder – it was the largest, the most glamorous, and soon to be the best known opera house in the world. There are countless rooms, halls all lavishly decorated in marble, the grandest of grand staircases and everywhere a profusion of embellishment: tapestries, sculptures, carvings, chandeliers, gilt and paintings.

The exterior of the building is no less splendid with one dominant and two lesser domes, six groups of angels surrounded by attendants, two winged horses, countless muses and cherubs, life-size statues and busts of composers, and numerous carved masks and medallions.

Opening night at the Palais Garnier was typically fraught: one of the main female singers

was ill, and so plans to perform entire acts of *Faust* and *Hamlet* were abandoned, leaving only a Delibes ballet and 'bleeding chunks' of *Les Huguenots* and *La Juive*. Notwithstanding this inauspicious start, Parisians flocked to the theatre, and money poured in to the box office.

Operatic novelty, however, was a little slow in coming, and when it did, French music continued to dominate: it was not until 1877 that the Opéra saw Massenet's *Le roi de Lahore* premièred. Wagner's music was still controversial: *Tannhäuser* had been booed off the stage, and performances of *Lohengrin* provoked a riot which the police had to suppress.

While international singers such as Nellie Melba, Jean de Reszke and Aïno Ackté joined the company in the early years of the 20th century, the particularly fierce brand of chauvinism continued from 1915 onwards. French singers, French opera, and French translations of foreign opera

dominated, and the Opéra's generally poor showing persisted until put smartly into reverse by the appointment of Rolf Liebermann in 1973; Liebermann and his music adviser Georg Solti, brought about the abandonment of the old permanent company and repertory system in favour of the more flexible *stagione* system.

It is probably fair to say that the work of Liebermann's successors, from 1980 onwards, was overshadowed by President Mitterrand's decision, in 1982, to build a new 'people's opera' – the Opéra Bastille. However, a consequence of the Opéra Bastille's troubled birth and persistent teething troubles has been the re-emergence of the Palais Garnier with the company's trouble-shooting director, Hugues Gall, appointed in 1994.

The architect: Charles Garnier
The building: Opened 1875
Capacity: About 2000
Opening perfomances: Selections from Meyerbeer's *Les Huguenots* and Halévy's *La Juive*
Innovation: Opera transmitted telephonically 1881
World première: Massenet's *Le roi de Lahore*

PARIS
OPÉRA COMIQUE

The Opéra Comique is not the oldest opera house in Paris, but it is the one most a part of Parisian daily life. Its origins lie in the entertainments offered to the populace on the streets, in particular during fairs, and mostly in the form of broad comedy, in the age-old form of mocking one's betters and parodying 'higher' concerns. By the 17th century, the court regularly visited these open-air entertainments. The original vaudeville, a song whose air had become common property, and to which new words – often on topical themes – were fitted, began here.

In 1642 Mazarin, as regent to the young Louis XIV, brought over a troupe of Italians, and soon 'the Italians' became a Parisian institution (no accident perhaps that the Opéra Comique is just off the boulevard des Italiens). Lully (an Italian let us not forget) began composing ballets for the court, and working with Molière. Gradually the influence of the fair made itself felt on these court amusements, and *vice versa*. The Italians also gave public performances of what we would today call revue, heavily laced with opera parodies.

After many vicissitudes in 1697 the Italians were expelled, ostensibly for the licentiousness of their performances, but really, so it was said, for having pilloried Madame de Maintenon in a piece called *La fausse prude*. Censorship only sharpened the wits of the fair-players, who eventually wore down the opposition, so that by the early 1700s fair-players were allowed into the Opéra (which, with the Comédie Française, had a legal monopoly on stage performances in Paris). It was at the Saint-Germain fair in 1715 that the name *opéra comique* appeared for the first time, as a narrative entertainment of songs and prose, the characters drawn from the traditional Italian figure of Harlequin, together with other stock: elderly husband, young lover, boastful Gascon, lawyer, priest.

In 1762 the Opéra Comique company entered its first permanent home, the Hôtel de Bourgogne, which soon proved inadequate, so finally a purpose-built theatre was constructed, opening in 1783, on the site of the present Opéra Comique. Burned down in 1838, a second theatre opened on the same site in 1840. This also burned down in 1887, and it is the third version, which opened in 1898, that we know today. Notwithstanding its incendiary progress in the 19th century, the Opéra Comique nevertheless achieved an incredible track record, particularly in French opera, with

The architect: Louis Bernier
The building: Opened 1898, as Salle Favart
Capacity: About 1300
World premières: Bizet's *Carmen*, 1875; Offenbach's *Les Contes d'Hoffmann*, 1881; Massenet's *Manon*, 1884; Debussy's *Pélleas et Mélisande*, 1902

premières of *Carmen*, *Les contes d'Hoffmann*, *Lakmé*, *Manon*, among many others, and first Paris productions of foreign work, ranging from Wagner to Puccini.

After having suffered a chequered career in the 20th century, including closure during the 1970s, the Opéra Comique has flourished, thanks in great part to the forceful character of its former director, Pierre Médecin, who returned the repertoire to the triumphs of the 19th century. The present director is Jeremy Savary, and under his leadership the Opéra Comique, remains very much the house for the locals.

Della Couling

Unlike the other opera houses in Paris, all occupying what the estate agents call commanding positions, the Opéra Comique is tucked away in a small square, the place Boieldieu, reached from a narrow side street, the rue Favart, off the boulevard des Italiens. These names are all significant; so many clues leading one to this particular opera house.

It was the Italians who first brought *commedia dell'arte* to Paris, that disrespectful, anarchic form of public entertainment that spawned the *opéra comique*, which began life as a lampoon of the high art of court-based opera, and developed into an art form of its own.

Charles Simon Favart (1710-1792) might now only have a side street named after him, but the rue Favart is the official address of the Opéra Comique (or Salle Favart, as it is once again known), as the administrative entrance to the building is on the rue Favart. Favart began his career in entertainment by writing vaudevilles – comic texts to well-known tunes, proceeding to full-length libretti (he wrote around 150 libretti for composers such as Grétry, Gluck and Philidor). He was one of those key figures who create a solid foundation for others to build on. From 1758 to 1769 he was the director of what in 1762 officially became the Opéra Comique, with its own building in the Hôtel de Bourgogne. It is fitting that the present theatre bears his name.

Poor old Adrien Boieldieu (1775-1834) is one of that sad legion of composers popular in their own time, now merely an unfamiliar name in gold lettering somewhere high up in the public spaces of an opera house, sandwiched tactlessly between Rossini and Bizet, as though to stress his present day obscurity. In the 1990s Pierre Médecin, the energetic intendant of the Opéra Comique, made amends by staging Boieldieu's acknowledged masterpiece, *La dame blanche*, which was premièred by the Opéra Comique – though not at its present home – in 1825.

And so we enter the house itself. Immediately confronting us are two stone statues at either side of the grand staircase: Massenet's Manon and Bizet's Carmen, both familiar and much-loved figures in French opera, both from operas premièred by the Opéra Comique.

Perhaps more than any other of the Parisian opera houses, there is a feeling at the Opéra Comique that this is the local, neighbourhood theatre. The atmosphere is relaxed and informal, even at premières, the public almost exclusively French. I was there in 1996 for a *Carmen*, directed by one-time intendant of the house, Louis Erlo (which got booed with great gusto at the end). Before the performance began, Pierre Médecin walked on to the stage to inform us there was a bomb scare, and would we please all go outside. Now I understand why *sang-froid* is a French expression: as the local Clouseau and his henchmen got to work inside searching for the (mythical) 'bomb', the audience, with good-nature and slightly amused exasperation, simply strolled out into the place Boieldieu and stood chatting amicably in the mild spring evening. One almost suspected some might have popped home for a quick coffee. After half an hour, back we trooped, past Manon and Carmen (both bombshells too in their time), to yet another rendition of that sublime work which has so often reverberated around this enchanting little theatre. Long may it continue to do so. And long may the audience boo or applaud, as they think fit.

QUESTA EFFIGIE
DI
GIOACCHINO ROSSINI
OPERA E GETTO
DI MAROCHETTI
GIUSEPPE DI SALAMANCA DI MADRID
GUSTAVO DELAHANTE DI PARIGI
DONARONO ALLA CITTÀ
DI PESARO
PATRIA DEL GRAN MAESTRO
LA QUALE
CON GRATO ANIMO E LIETA POMPA
LA INAUGURAVA
IL XXI AGOSTO MDCCCLXIV

PESARO
TEATRO ROSSINI

An Adriatic resort whose heyday was in the 19th century, when Caroline, Princess of Wales, had a villa there, Pesaro still manages to muster some of its old sense of cultivation and respectability, despite being under siege from package tourism.

The Teatro Rossini, too, is something of a grand old dame, but one who was so shaky that she very nearly didn't survive. The theatre was built, probably too hastily, in 1818 to plans by Pietro Ghinelli – a local follower of Giuseppe Piermarini, who had designed Milan's La Scala – where the Teatro del Sole had been since 1637, and before that the site of the stables of the noble Della Rovere family. Traces of the family can still be found over the present theatre's doorway. Inside, the Rossini follows the classic horseshoe plan, with four tiers, a ceiling decorated with painted scenes of dancing muses, and the original, Neo-Classical curtain.

For the inauguration, Rossini, the great maestro himself, is chronicled as having stood at the podium at the age of only twenty-six to conduct a new version of his opera *La gazza ladra*, which he had composed the year before and had just revised for the occasion. Born in 1792, in a house that is now a museum on a street that bears his name, the composer, as everyone will remind you, was Pesaro's own son. Although his memories of the theatre were not always rosy, especially just after the inauguration, it was renamed the Teatro Rossini

following major repairs in 1855. When he died thirteen years later, Rossini surprised everyone by leaving his entire fortune to Pesaro. The legacy was used to start both the Rossini Foundation and a conservatory, which soon gained a world-wide reputation.

But the theatre fared less well. Several earthquakes required further extensive repairs. Then,

---

The architect: Pietro Ghinelli
The building: Opened 1818; closed as unsafe 1966, reopened 1980, since then the venue for the annual Rossini festival
Capacity: About 900
Opening perfomance: Rossini's *La gazza ladra*, conducted by the composer
World premières: Mascagni's *Zanetton*, 1896; Zandonai's *La Via della Finestra*, 1919

in 1966, due to neglect and, apparently, shoddy building practices, even back in 1818, the Teatro Rossini was declared unsafe and shut down. Still more major renovations ensued. It reopened in 1980. The same year the Rossini Opera Festival was born. A key fixture on the world opera circuit, it takes place every August and is the only international event dedicated to the composer's prolific output. These productions are not only meant to entertain, but also to contribute to a project begun in 1974 to publish a critical, ninety-volume edition of Rossini's complete works, some of which are still unknown.

Bruce Johnston on Pesaro, Rossini and Luciano Pavarotti

Although Rossini has given his name to the house and street where he was born, to Pesaro's opera house, to the foundation begun with the money he left to the town, and to the annual opera festival, the truth is that, when he was alive, Rossini chose not to linger very long in Pesaro. He left in a hurry to pursue his extraordinary career and rarely returned. Yet in modern times – although there are no sign-posts to testify to the fact – another opera figure, who has probably already become a much greater legend in his own lifetime, has made Pesaro his adoptive home, one to which he returns from venues around the world to escape the frantic rush of an equally extraordinary career.

Yet, surely, there is some operatic irony in the fact that this newcomer – a tenor, who is unquestionably the greatest voice of his day – should have come to the one place in the world that is so totally identified by the one composer whose works he cannot, by his own admission, sing.

For, as Luciano Pavarotti sighed: 'It's not that I don't love Rossini, but rather, that Rossini doesn't love me. Or, better still, that he doesn't love *my* voice. For his operas, my voice is no good. The only exception is *Guglielmo Tell*. But that's gruelling . . .'

The irony is heightened further by the fact that it was none other than Pavarotti, then already something of a local personality as well as a celebrated singer the world over, who was asked in 1980 to sing in a gala concert to mark the reopening of the Teatro Rossini.

It is difficult to imagine such an inauguration without something on the programme by Rossini. If there wasn't, few if anyone would have known why. And if there was, then who may ever know with what suffering it was sung? And of those who knew, how many realised?

But Pavarotti did not come to Pesaro for opera. He knew it as a seaside resort when he was a teenager, and he returned to it as a seaside resort later on. Locals like to stress that there is more to Pesaro than just the sea. And at Pavarotti's home, of course, there is also music. Lots of it. There is a piano – 'I have pianos everywhere, without them I am lost'. And there, possibly whilst lounging in a hammock, and after a spell in the pool, he pours over his operatic roles for the coming season – but please, no Rossini!

PRAGUE
Opera Houses: Brendan Carroll

Prague was a sleeping city for over half a century, during the occupation by both Nazi and Communist forces, and its recent re-emergence into the modern world has been traumatic. It survived World War II unscathed and has been largely untouched by development – yet a clash of post-war western culture with what remains essentially an 18th century city has meant that its unique atmosphere has been somewhat disturbed in recent years. However, for the intrepid music lover, a visit to Prague out of season (October until early April) will still be a magical experience and fortunately coincides with the height of its opera season.

The operatic tradition of Prague stretches back to the 17th century, but for most visitors it is its association with Mozart which is paramount. Indeed, it remains the most important Mozart shrine outside of Salzburg. The Stavovské Divadlo (Estates Theatre) is now the only surviving theatre where Mozart worked. For the visitor, the surrounding area is the perfect setting, with Mozart's apartment just a few steps away and three doors down the home of Schikaneder (the instigator of *Die Zauberflöte*) still stands. Its exterior is one of the most graceful Neo-Classical buildings in Europe.

The repertoire of this theatre used to be proscribed by the Communist authorities to offer only modern, politically correct works. Since 1989, it has thankfully returned to being a Baroque theatre with matching repertoire, and gradually it is restoring its former eminence in performing 18th and early 19th century opera. Because of its historical significance tickets are almost impossible to obtain unless booked well in advance.

In complete contrast, the Národní Divadlo (National Theatre) is conceived on a much grander scale and dates from the 1880s, a superb example of the high Neo-Renaissance style. It overlooks the River Vltava and like the Estates Theatre it, too, underwent extensive restoration in the 1970s and 1980s. Both its interior and exterior are lavishly appointed and its gilded auditorium boasts exceptionally fine acoustics, although given the scale of the building, it holds surprisingly few. Sitting amidst the lavish splendour, one can easily conjure up images of the great musicians of the past who stood before the richly embroidered curtains: Smetana, Dvořák, Suk and even Richard Strauss, who conducted his revolutionary opera *Elektra* here in 1910, not long after its première in Dresden. An inscribed score is preserved in the archives.

The best time to see these exceptionally beautiful buildings is early in the morning, before the streets are thronged with visitors. The Stavovské Divadlo in particular, is situated in an irresistibly romantic setting in a little square, surrounded by a rabbit-warren of connecting streets, although some modern development nearby is threatening to mar this. It is still possible to imagine that one sees Mozart – frock coat open, cane in hand, rushing up the stairs to the mezzanine floor on the outside of this charming theatre – late for rehearsals.

As one approaches the epic proportions of the Národní Divadlo, the age of the grandiloquent carriage trade returns, as in former times the aristocracy of *fin de siècle* Prague arrived here in style at the splendid porticoed entrance to hear the great Emmy Destinnova.

PRAGUE
NÁRODNÍ DIVADLO

P rague's imposing National Theatre (Národní Divadlo) was built to designs by Josef Zitek in 1881, and paid for by public subscription. With a capacity of 1,500 and a stage measuring 22 by 20 metres, the theatre incorporated the much smaller stage of the 1862 Královské Zemské České Divadlo (Royal Provincial Czech Theatre); this predecessor theatre – known as the Provisional Theatre – had played host, in 1866, to the première of *The Bartered Bride* by Smetana, who was chief conductor from 1874 to 1881. It was fitting, therefore, that the inaugural production at the splendid new National Theatre should be another première by the country's foremost composer, Smetana: *Libuše*. The original Národní Divadlo proved to the be short-lived. Two months after the première of *Libuše,* the theatre burnt down, to reopen in 1883.

The structure of the building survived the fire, unlike its architect who was replaced by his pupil Josef Schulz, who supervised the reconstruction. The theatre stands on an imposing site by the River Vltava; the main façade has Corinthian pillars over the arched porch, statues of the Muses, and two horse-drawn chariots driven by winged figures of Victory.

Between 1888 and 1918, Czech composers featured prominently. Among the many premières were Fibich's *The Bride of Messina* (1884), Šmetana's *Dalibor* (1886), Dvořák's *The Jacobin* (1889) and *Eva* (1899) by Josef Foerster. While the number of performances by Smetana dwarfed those of other composers, Verdi, Wagner and Mozart were regularly performed. The National Theatre was the Czech showcase *par excellence*, and

composers continued to provide it with operas commensurate with its international standing: Dvořák's last operas, *Rusalka* (1901) and *Armida* (1904), Janáček's *The Excursions of Mr Brouček* (1920) and Martinů's *Julietta* (1938) were all premièred there.

During the reconstruction of the National Theatre from 1977 to 1983, a new stage (Nová Scéna) was added for drama and chamber opera. The National Theatre has continued in its commitment to present new Czech opera under such conductors as Chalabala, Krombholc, Košler and producer Kašlík.

The architect: Josef Zitek
The building: Opened 1881; fire damage two months later, reopened 1883
Capacity: About 1500
Opening perfomance: Smetana's *Libuše*
World première: Dvořák's *Rusalka*, 1901

PRAGUE
STAVOVSKÉ DIVADLO

One of the few 18th century theatres still in use as an opera house, the Stavovské Divadlo is famous for Mozart conducting *Don Giovanni* in 1787 and *La clemenza di Tito* in 1791. It is also, confusingly, famous for being known variously as the Gräflich Nostitzsche Nationaltheater, the Tyl Theater and now, reopened after a long and thorough restoration, as the Stavovské Divadlo (Estates Theatre).

The architect Anton Haffenecker designed the building which opened in April 1783 with a performance of *Emilia Galotti* by Lessing. The theatre's original layout allowed over one thousand people to be accommodated, but with several reconstructions the auditorium today has only about three hundred seats. The latest restoration of this elegant Baroque theatre with Corinthian pillars, green painted walls and steep red-tiled roof is one of the sights visitors come to see in this splendid city.

Mozart would recognise the façade of the building which has changed little since his première of *Don Giovanni*. He returned to the theatre in 1791 to conduct the first performance of his final opera *La clemenza di Tito*, commissioned by Leopold II for his coronation as King of Bohemia. Soon after, in December 1791, Mozart died in Vienna.

After a spell of German operas introduced by Carl Maria von Weber, the nationalist fervour of the 19th century encouraged performances in the Czech language and the first Czech opera, *Drátenik*, by František Škroup (1826).

With the appointment in 1846 of Josef Kajetan Tyl (who gave his name to the theatre for a time), production in Czech continued with notable performances in translation of Verdi's *Nabucco*.

The turmoil of the 20th century is reflected in the history of the house in which the tastes and preferences of the various occupiers of the country had to be followed.

Now Mozart's operas are back and audiences can enjoy the performances in the faithfully restored theatre just as it was at the first performance of *Don Giovanni* conducted by Wolfgang Amadeus Mozart over two hundred years ago.

The architect: Anton Haffenecker
The building: Opened 1783
Capacity: About 300
Opening perfomance: Lessing's *Emilia Galotti*
World première: Mozart's *Don Giovanni* conducted by the composer

REGGIO EMILIA
IL TEATRO MUNICIPALE VALLI

Built to replace the Teatro Pubblico in the Cittadella which had been destroyed by fire, the Municipale opened, 'bigger and better', as promised, in 1857 with a production of the opera *Vittore Pisani*, set to music by Achille Peri, a Reggio native. It was renamed in 1980 after Romolo Valli, a local actor.

Opera first developed in Florence around 1600, and in the next fifty years appeared elsewhere, especially Cremona and Mantua, and above all Venice, where it took on the form with which we are familiar today. The fertile and creative region of Emilia Romagna, where Reggio is found, is central to and borders on the regions of all these cities. Opera, music, drama, and, more recently, dance, all enjoy strong traditions in Emilia

Romagna, which is where the composer Giuseppe Verdi and Luciano Pavarotti, the tenor, were both born. In 1961, as part of the first international competition for singing, the winner Luciano Pavarotti made his début at the Valli singing the role of Rodolfo in *La bohème*.

A Neo-Classical gem which is large, yet graceful, the Valli faces south, its main façade comprised of a portico supported by twelve columns and reached by three granite steps. Above, fourteen Ionic pilasters divide thirteen windows, while crowning the front of the building are fourteen statues. From left to right they represent Tragedy, Vice, Glory, Drama, Virtue, Truth, Learning, Teaching, Fable, Satire, Dance, Inspiration, Comedy and Music. Three other statues top each side elevation, and another four adorn each of the side terraces.

Inside, the horseshoe-shaped auditorium is resplendent in white with gold filigree, with an extensive stage, four tiers of 106 boxes – in the middle of which, in the second tier, is the Ducal (later Royal) Box – and the *loggione*.

In the past, this was a theatre that was more than happy to stick where possible to popular opera successes of the *La Traviata*, *Rigoletto*, and *La bohème* variety, rather than to chance unorthodox works. Then, in the late 1950s, a kind of Renaissance occurred. Between 1957 and 1980, the theatre's repertoire had so widened that of the 107 operas produced, 67 had never been seen there before. Many pre-dated the Romantic period, or were contemporary, foreign, or minor Italian works from the 19th century. At about the same time, the Municipale and, as a result, Reggio Emilia in general, began to get an international reputation as being an important venue for dance, especially after the mid-1960s when the theatre's number of annual ballet productions all at once doubled.

The architect: Cesare Costa
The building: Opened 1857
Capacity: About 1200
Opening perfomance: Peri's *Vittore Pisani*
Notable appearance: Luciano Pavarotti débuted as Rodolfo in *La bohème*, 1961

Bruce Johnston

Just as La Scala's special magic is to be found well within that theatre, that of the Valli in Reggio is, if anything, outside. It isn't that the interior is uneventful. And operas in Reggio have a tradition for pleasing the eye. It is only that the monumental quality of the Valli's exterior, and the mixture of delicacy and power of its situation, is such that it is not easy to shake off when you go inside.

It seems to set the mood of performances, and even of the town. For although this left-leaning, provincial capital is stocked with Renaissance and Baroque churches and palaces, the opera house – which is Neo-Classical, and of a warm, terracotta colour, in contrast to the more melancholy hues of La Scala – is undoubtedly Reggio's high-point. Any major world city would be more than pleased to have the Valli. But when it was built, Reggio, a mainly agricultural town, had barely 15,000 inhabitants.

My first experience of this remarkable theatre was to happen upon it at night, and in the dead of winter, when the town was shrouded in an insidious and thick, freezing fog. The performance had long before ended, but the effect was equally dramatic.

Upon entering an immense piazza, which is really two piazzas in one, and where the army used to exercise, there, out of the pea-soup, loomed the Teatro Valli like a ghost-ship bearing down in the night, and apparently emitting steam.

There was no traffic. To the right were trees, shadows, steps, a war monument to the Partisans, and a church and a large museum. In front of the theatre, an uninspiring fountain, and the Piazza dei Martiri (Square of the Martyrs). It is named after workers who were killed by police – not one hundred years ago or so as you might expect, but in 1960 – for demonstrating against an attempted, right-wing coup. To the left, the square continues, but is renamed – yes, Piazza della Libertà.

There, behind a 'Monument to the Fallen', sits a magical park, against whose limes, and squat, ancient cedars that groan with the weight of the ages, is silhouetted part of the profile of the opera house. If trees have spirits, they are here.

This would have been a strong enough image if that had been all. But, incredibly, to the left of these gardens, where the branches and trunks have turned fat from pruning, I all at once perceived not just one but two more theatres looming out of the winter vapour: the Ariosto, built in 1878, and the Cavallerizza, a more recent and interesting theatre created out of old stables used by the lancers. After encountering imagery such as that, an opera seems almost futile.

Cristina Grimandi
Opera houses in Italy through the eyes of a child

In 1971 I was at the School of Antoniano in Bologna under the direction of Olga Olgiati (dancer of La Scala in Milan between the wars with Cecchetti). I was chosen to be the child in the productions of *Le baiser de la fée* and *Pulcinella* by Igor Stravinsky. The first ballerina was Carla Fracci. I would watch her in her solitary warm-up; always wearing a jacket, with a sheer skirt to the knees and very big leg warmers.

One day at rehearsal the stage manager couldn't find the prop for me so the director Beppe Menegatti threw me his shoes instead. 'She's going to die!' screamed choreographer Loris Gaj with laughter. I thought, in fact, 'A nice colour, but what a smell!' I lived, however, and the première was on 23 November 1971 in the Teatro Comunale di Bologna. It was a big success: 'Brava', 'Bis'. The audience was enthusiastic and I remember lots of flowers flying on stage from everywhere! On 20 January 1972 we had our second première at La Fenice in Venice.

There was a very nice restaurant in the piazzetta where most of the artists would eat before and after the show. I found a friend there, about my age, and his mother was wearing a big black fur that she threw over a chair. She was also working in the theatre in the production of Catalani's *La Wally*. I saw her signing lots of autographs and when we were playing together, running around the tables in the restaurant, she was calling to my friend, 'Nino, veni aqui!' She was Montserrat Caballé.

The production moved down to the Teatro Comunale in Florence. I was going to school every morning in my home town. The days we had a performance, I would take the train with my father at 2 p.m. to be in Florence in time for the rehearsal and show. I always had with me my dance shoes and homework. I was usually stretching in the ballet room with the company and then studying maths and grammar in my dressing room.

One day in Florence I had permission to watch the run-through of *Cavalleria rusticana* from the first row. 'What a voice,' I thought. That day I decided to be a singer like Gianni Poggi the tenor. A very nice lady tried to stop me running down the stairs one night. I had to catch the train at 1.30 a.m. back to Bologna with my father. She couldn't stop me but I heard a voice saying, 'I saw the performance, you moved me very much!' That was the voice of Giulietta Simionato.

The tour continued through the cities of Parma, Ferrara and Reggio Emilia. During the tour I also met one of the greatest tenors of the century. At the time I didn't know his name but I remember a lot of people watching him with his big foulard draped over his shoulders. Luciano Pavarotti turned around and smiled at me before he walked out of the stage door.

The last performance was in the Teatro Consorziale in Budrio. As the curtains closed I felt an emptiness and the end of a dream. In almost eight months I had saved enough money to buy a piano and I made my biggest decision, that I will continue to work in the theatre.

SALZBURG
GROSSES FESTSPIELHAUS

Possessing a rich and illustrious history of performing arts which dates from the early 17th century, Salzburg is the obvious city to host probably the greatest annual music festival in the world. Mozart, as a favourite son, served as an inspiration to the cause as early as 1842 with the unveiling of a monument to the great composer by Ludwig Schwanthaler. Until World War I the festival took place on an occasional basis. On 22 August 1920 it opened with Hugo von Hofmannsthal's *Jedermann*.

The nucleus of the three performance halls lies in the 17th-century royal stable block that now contains the various foyers. The building was first adapted for current use by Eduard Hütter then redesigned by Clemens Holzmeister in the 1920s and the theatre, seating nearly 1,400, became known as the Kleines Festspielhaus in the 1930s. Meanwhile another renovation in the same complex, the Felsenreitschule (Riding School) provides seating for over 1,500 and staged its first opera in 1948. Originally an amphitheatre with a dramatic backdrop arcade of spectator boxes designed by Fischer von Erlach which had been cut into the rock during the 17th century, the auditorium was remodelled in 1968 to shield the audience from the elements.

In order to meet demand, Holzmeister was also responsible for the design of a third theatre in the complex which began in 1956. The Grosses Festspielhaus, seating nearly 3,500, took four years to build and involved blasting 55,000 cubic yards of rock from the side of the adjacent Mönchsberg. Architectural features include frescoes, bronze and boiserie doors and panels, mosaics, tapestries, Murano glass sconces illuminating Carrara marble sculptures of Music and Theatre – all contribute to adorn this palace of music which is an interesting mix from four centuries of architectural design.

During the first two decades of the festival the music was dominated by the works of Mozart and Strauss with an occasional piece by Gluck. Although the festival managed to continue during World War II, its activities were severely curtailed. The première of Strauss's *Die Liebe der Danae*, conducted by Clemens Krauss, was scheduled for 1944, but following the D-Day invasion Goebbels ordered all German and Austrian theatres to be closed. However, a local governor allowed rehearsals to continue. During one highly-charged rehearsal of the second scene of Act III, Strauss got to his feet and approached the orchestra rail; at the end, there was a long silence after which conductor Clemens Krauss said a few words, then Strauss, thanking the orchestra in a voice choked with tears, said: 'Perhaps we shall meet

again in a better world.' Strauss stood throughout the last scene; tearful at the end. He refused to sanction a further performance in his lifetime. By 1952, when the opera was finally performed in Salzburg, Strauss had died.

In 1967 Herbert von Karajan initiated an Easter Festival to complement the Summer Festival and both regularly see performances by outstanding conductors and singers. In 1991, artistic director Gerard Mortier was appointed to initiate a programme dominated by modern and classical works to the same extent.

The architect: Clemens Holzmeister
The building: Opened 1960
Capacity: About 3500
Opening performance: Richard Strauss's *Der Rosenkavalier*

SAN FRANCISCO
WAR MEMORIAL OPERA HOUSE

The first opera heard in the city was Bellini's *La Sonnambula,* performed by the Pellegrini troupe in 1851 at the Adelphi Theater. The following decades saw thousands of performances for the enthusiastic and passionate music lovers of the city, in many theatres, by many touring companies, including several visits by the New York Metropolitan Opera performing Verdi's *Otello, Il Travatore* and, in 1900, Wagner's *Ring.* Only hours after Enrico Caruso and Olive Fremstad stopped singing in *Carmen,* the 1906 earthquake struck and devastated the opera house and most of the city.

The San Francisco Opera Company was founded in 1923, but it was not until the 1930s, when veterans of World War I decided to commemorate their service to their country, and raised the necessary funds for building a new opera house. The classical Baroque design by the architect Arthur Brown was opened in 1932, with a performance of Puccini's *Tosca.* The building forms part of the Civic Center Complex, including the Museum of Modern Art. In 1979 the backstage was enlarged and an additional wing was built to house rehearsal studios and stages.

The War Memorial Opera House, with a capacity of about 3000, is open again after work to repair the damage caused by the 1989 earthquake. The adventurous programmes nowadays are sometimes broadcast live to several States, and the company travels to communities with full-length productions, as well as providing live entertainment in everyday locations by the Brown Bag Opera Company.

The architects: Arthur Brown, G. Albert Lansburgh, Willis Polk
The building: Opened 1932; earthquake 1989, reopened 1998
Capacity: About 3000
Opening perfomance: Puccini's *Tosca*

STOCKHOLM
KUNGLIGA TEATERN

In 1773 Gustavus III, cultural patron and playwright, converted some real tennis courts to create an opera house. That year it saw the première of the first opera in Swedish, *Thetis and Pelée* by Francesco Uttini. In 1782 a new purpose-built opera house opened, designed by Carl Fredrik Adelcrantz and described as one of Europe's most beautiful.

The opera by J.G. Naumann, *Cora and Alonzo,* opened the new theatre and his *Gustaf Wasa* in 1786 became a great success of the period.

The 19th century produced Sweden's most distinguished composer, Franz Berwald and many notable singers like his pupil Christine Nilsson, and Jenny Lind, the 'Swedish nightingale'. The present theatre was built on the site of the older one demolished in 1891. The Neo-Classical building was designed by Axel Anderberg, a solid edifice by the Norrbro bridge in the centre of town.

The first opera specially written for the Royal Opera House was Hallén's *Waldemarsskatten* performed in 1899. Stockholm's first *Ring* cycle in 1907 ushered in a period of Wagner productions and the emergence of many Wagnerian singers of quality including Set Svanholm, Nanny Larsén-Todsen, Birgit Nilsson, Berit Lindholm and Helge Brilioth. Today singers like MariAnne Häggander and Gösta Winbergh are carrying on the tradition.

Many former singers, according to tradition, became directors of the opera until 1952 when the remarkable director Göran Gentele took control. He was responsible for many new productions including in 1958 his innovative *Un ballo in maschera* with a bisexual Gustavus III. This production toured to London, Montreal and Edinburgh and has often been revived.

The Royal Opera continued to produce excellent home-grown singers after the war, among them Elisabeth Söderström, Jussi Björling, Nicolai Gedda and Kerstin Meyer – who became director of the Royal Opera School.

The Royal Opera in Stockholm celebrated its two hundredth anniversary in 1973 with Werle's *Tintomara*. György Ligeti wrote a new opera for the theatre in 1978: *Le grand macabre* was a controversial yet successful work,

produced by the director of Stockholm's puppet theatre, Michael Meschke. A notable world première was Ingvar Lidholm's *A Dream Play* in 1992.

The Kungliga Teatern is the home of the country's oldest and largest orchestra – the Royal Orchestra – together with the Royal Opera Chorus and the Royal Opera Ballet. As an ensemble company it maintains some forty resident soloists, and continues to nurture native talent and set a high standard in production of old and new works.

The architect: Axel Anderberg
The building: Opened 1898; Gustavus III assassinated in previous opera house in 1792, an event recorded in Verdi's *Un Ballo in Maschera*
Capacity: About 1200
Opening perfomance: Berwald's *Estrella de Soria*
World première: Lindholms' *A Dream Play* 1992

STOCKHOLM
DROTTNINGHOLM

Drottningholm, or Queen's Island, has been the summer residence of the ladies of the Swedish court for four hundred years. It was the custom to present the palace and its environs to the young bride who came to marry the Swedish Crown Prince. Thus it was in 1744 that Frederick I made a wedding present of the royal country residence to Princess Louisa Ulrica of Prussia, sister of Frederick the Great, on the occasion of her betrothal to the Swedish heir apparent, Adolf Fredrik.

The union was celebrated with due pomp and ceremony, and as part of the wedding festivities a group of Swedish actors came to the island to perform. Louisa Ulrica was evidently accustomed to more sophisticated entertainment and so she had the whole lot cashiered and replaced in 1753 by a troupe from Paris, some 150 individuals in all who were housed in the theatre itself (a not uncommon practice in the theatres of the period) which was built on the north side of the courtyard at Drottningholm palace at Louisa Ulrica's instigation.

The existing theatre is, in fact, the second theatre on the site, rising Phoenix-like out of the ashes of its predecessor, which was completely destroyed by fire in 1762. It is a lasting testament to the skills of Louisa Ulrica's new troupe that when a female member of the cast came rushing on to the stage yelling, 'Le feu! le feu!' and fainted, she was fervently applauded by the audience which fondly imagined that this was all part of the new style of acting. The present theatre was designed by the architect Carl Fredrik Adelcrantz and work was completed in 1766. It was to be twice as big as the old theatre.

The auditorium is divided into three sections, mapping out the demarcation lines between royalty, nobility and the servant classes. The Royal Boxes (one on each side of the auditorium) are hardly ever used these days because they are so small.

The entire theatre is just one big set-piece, like an 18th century version of a Pollock's toy theatre writ large. The solid-looking edifice is made entirely of wood with a thin plaster skim. Ornate cornices are in fact elaborately moulded papier mâché and the ceiling (largely responsible for the unbelievable acoustics) is cunningly painted wood which, although completely flat, contrives to resemble stucco mouldings.

The modern visitor must accustom his eyes to candle power before this *trompe-l'oeil* is

revealed. Wax tapers were replaced by electric replicas some twenty years ago, while the candles in operation in the auditorium today, although readily available world-wide these days, were invented specifically for Drottningholm's auditorium.

The whole theatre has been compared by former artistic director Elisabeth Söderström to 'a Stradivarius. Drottningholm is the only place in the world where we can give a full-blown 18th century performance.' There are, of course, drawbacks to opening the theatre

---

The architect: Carl Frederik Adelcrantz
The building: Opened 1764; closed after the assassination of Gustavus III in 1792; rediscovered and reopened 1922
Capacity: About 454

to the general public. According to conductor Nicholas McGegan 'the interior décor of the auditorium is falling apart'. Backstage, however, wear-and-tear is not in evidence. The stage equipment appears to be in a high state of preservation thanks in part to the genius of its creator, an Italian stage mechanic named Donato Stopany, who worked with Adelcrantz to create a system of stage machinery which is awe-inspiring even by today's standards. The stage – 20 metres from footlights to back wall – is one of Sweden's deepest. The machinery for effecting scene changes – a system of windlass, trolleys and pulleys – makes comparison between the theatre and some great sailing ship inevitable. Within a matter of seconds a thirty-man stage crew can turn Elysium to Hades (subject of course, to the demands of the director), an achievement that cannot even be emulated by Covent Garden.

There is a manually operated wave machine which creates on-stage undulations and an exact replica of the Swedish fleet which emerges to do battle as required. Two chariots (large and small) descend from the fly floor to provide greater and lesser deities with their means of transport in vast cloud banks which cosmetically conceal their flying apparatus. A variety of trap doors allow the denizens of Hell to make their appearance or, of course, the more egregious sinners of the operatic stage to be swallowed up. There is an equally magnificent and unique collection of fifteen stage sets complete with backcloths, wings and flies together with a further twenty incomplete sets. These days the scenery in use on the stage is an exact replica of the originals as the possibility of inflicting irreparable damage to 18th century fabric proved too real a danger.

Much has been made of Louisa Ulrica's involvement with the theatre, indeed she presides nightly over proceedings – depicted in the form of the goddess Minerva on the stage curtain, but the theatre was at its heyday during the reign of Gustavus III. If his name sounds familiar, he's the one who in 1792 met an untimely death from an assassin's bullet during a masked ball at the Kungliga Teatern (immortalised by Verdi in *Un ballo in maschera*). He was the 18th century epitome of the Renaissance ideal of the 'complete' man – playwright, author, actor, director, politician, philosopher and architect. He is also unique among monarchs in having an opera style (Gustavian) named after him.

The theatre closed after the assassination and fell into disuse. It began to be used as a lumber-room by palace servants who filled it with furniture and old carpets, transforming it into an extremely well kept secret until its rediscovery in the 1920s. Agne Beijer, then a student, was researching a lost painting, took a wrong turning and stumbled upon it by accident. As his eyes grew accustomed to the gloom, he realised that he was on stage. His lucky find has enabled generations of theatre-goers to share in the incalculable privilege and pleasures of visiting this unique theatre where every evening's entertainment is a piece of living history.

There can be no possible disappointment in a visit to Drottningholm, surely one of the most beautiful opera houses on earth. A small, 18th century jewel of a theatre, it is part of the royal cluster of buildings near Stockholm that the Swedes liken to the royal splendour of Versailles.

Andrew Parrott

To perform bewigged and in 18th-century royal servant's costume is not something that is often required of me as a conductor. Yet such is the enchantment of Drottningholm's court theatre that any self-consciousness vanishes almost at once and the spectacle of similarly-attired orchestral players, huddled together hard up against the front of the stage, soon becomes the most natural thing in the world.

Indeed, as the theatre's unostentatious exterior itself implies, there is nothing at all precious about the Drottningholm experience. Sitting comfortably at the less formal edge of the palace gardens and just a few hundred yards from the main part of the palace, the building wears its historical importance and its uniqueness lightly. (Within ten minutes of arriving there for the first time, a visiting pupil of mine managed by pure chance not only to see but to meet the King of Sweden!)

Inside, in the glow of (meticulously simulated) candlelight, Drottningholm's irresistible magic really begins to tell. Proceedings begin, conventionally enough, with the conductor's entrance – but heralded here by an imposing three-fold knocking on the wooden floor. (One production – of Pergolesi's *La serva padrona* – required me, rather less ceremoniously, to launch precipitously into the first aria after hurrying through the darkened auditorium and vaulting into the orchestra.) Clearly, the spectacle is a principal delight, but for performers and audience alike the theatre proves equally generous to the ear; the wooden construction lends a supportive warmth to the sound, and the human scale of the auditorium (seating no more than four hundred or so) allows an exceptional intimacy in which both singers (and words) can project with absolute ease, and stage and band can interact as in chamber music-making.

All this is utterly spoiling. I don't know of another opera house in which – not least in purely musical terms – the 18th-century repertory is so effortlessly at home. Also, by virtue of functioning for only part – the warmer part – of each year and of playing leisurely host to a few productions at a time, the theatre seems to lead a charmed existence, blissfully innocent of the routine pressures that can weigh down bigger and busier operatic institutions and the sensitive souls within them. May Drottningholm survive at least another two hundred years and more, as a model of the sort of house in which the earlier operatic repertory can thrive, true to itself.

STUTTGART
WÜRTTEMBERGISCHES STAATSTHEATER

With German opera all but non-existent in late 17th-century Stuttgart, visiting Italian companies were in constant demand. By the mid-18th century, French and Italian variants of *opera seria* and *opera buffa* along with German *Singspiel* were performed on a regular basis. Thanks to the enthusiastic patronage of Duke Carl Eugen, Stuttgart's new converted Hoftheater opened in 1750. With others keen to put the city on the musical map, it was soon enjoying mainstream productions, eventually seeing the likes of *Die Zauberflöte* (1795) and *Don Giovanni* (1796). As is often the case, the death of the aristocratic patron, Carl Eugen, was followed by a decline in the quality of opera in Stuttgart.

Various directors in the first half of the 19th century encouraged a revival of operatic fortunes by featuring such composers as Weber (who worked as ducal secretary from 1807 to 1810) and Beethoven. The city was further distinguished by the presence of Meyerbeer directing his own *L'étoile du nord* and *Dinorah* in 1854 and 1859 respectively.

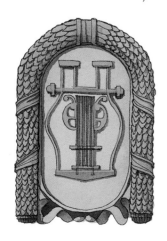

A new musical director, Max von Schillings, was appointed in 1908 and this led to the opening of a new two-theatre complex, built by architect Max Littmann 1909-12. The austere Classical façade has a rounded portico of giant order Ionic columns erected in pairs. The attic storey behind the open balustrade supports a series of full-length classical figures forming a silhouette reminiscent of Palladio's Villa Chiericati in Vicenza.

The Kleines Haus opened in 1912 with the world première of *Ariadne auf Naxos* conducted by the composer, Richard Strauss. Von Schillings premièred his *Mona Lisa* in 1915. Subsequent directors were responsible for the productions of works by Hindemith, Pfitzner and Stravinsky, and complete Weber and Wagner cycles.

Following World War II, the theatre reopened in 1946 with Germany's first performance of Hindemith's *Mathis der Maler*, previously banned by the Nazis. The house continues its reputation for works by Strauss, Wagner and contemporary operas regularly featuring some of the best of German performers.

The architect: Max Littmann
The building: Opened 1912
Capacity: About 1400
Opening perfomance and world première: Strauss's *Ariadne auf Naxos* conducted by the composer

SYDNEY
OPERA HOUSE

Like the Statue of Liberty to New York, and the Eiffel Tower to Paris, the Opera House has become the immediately recognisable symbol of Sydney. The history of this most unusual structure is as exciting as the silhouette of the building beside the Harbour Bridge. It was built on Bennelong Point to the design of a Danish architect, Jørn Utzon, winner of the design competition announced by the government of New South Wales in 1955 and awarded, in 1957, on the basis of some rather sketchy, but

revolutionary designs. There followed a turbulent period of some eighteen years, the resignation of Utzon, the appointment of structural engineers Ove Arup to make the structure stand up, and the appointment of the architect Peter Hall to lead a team to redesign the interior and finish the project. The complex has a Concert Hall with a capacity of 2,600, and a smaller Opera Theatre with 1,500 seats, as well as three more smaller halls. Queen Elizabeth II opened the Opera House in October 1973 and eight days later the first performance was Prokofiev's opera *War and Peace* conducted by Edward Dawnes.

The turbulent times continued after the completion of the complex, with the management of the Australian Opera, where general managers did not last long, and morale and finances suffered. Toward the end of the 1980s the first native Australian, Donald McDonald, was appointed general manager.

The architect: Jorn Utzon
The building: Opened 1973
Capacity: About 2600 and 1500 in the two main theatres
Opening perfomance: Prokofiev's *War and Peace*
Notable appearances: Joan Sutherland in Léhar's *The Merry Widow*, her husband Richard Bonynge conducting 1978

Gordon French

Being an Australian, and from time to time living and working in London, returning to Sydney is always an emotional experience. As the aircraft makes its final approach into Sydney the sight of the Opera House glinting in the sunlight on Bennelong Point makes the hair on the back of your neck stand on end.

On a visit back to Sydney in 1999 my family and I attended a performance of *Madam Butterfly*. The production was outstanding and at the interval, to walk out on the concourse and enjoy the lights of the city and bridge reflected in the harbour is an experience impossible to put into words.

My first visit to the Opera House was in August 1974 – one year after it had opened. Leonard Bernstein brought the New York Philharmonic to Australia – Bernstein wanted to experience the new hall's acoustics. After complaining about the ticket prices he gave a free performance of Tchaikovsky's 6th Symphony, the Pathétique, in the morning for his young fans – an unbelievable event. Three days later, I recorded a television interview with him and Margaret Whitlam, wife of the then Australian Prime Minister, in Melbourne. He was still raving about the hall and the reaction to the performance.

The Merry Widow was my first opera at the House in 1978, with Dame Joan Sutherland, and Richard Bonynge conducting. Staged in the Concert Hall on an elegant set by Kristian Fredrikson, the season was a sell-out and Brian Hoad from *The Bulletin* wrote: '[Sutherland's] sense of fun is irresistibly contagious, her warmth is palpable, her romantic affectations naively touching and sincere and she sings like the legendary pontevedrian nightingale'. I could not have put it better!

VENICE
TEATRO LA FENICE

On 29 January 1996, during closure for repairs, Venice's La Fenice opera house burned down in what magistrates believe was an arson attack. Suspicions have fallen on contractors and mafia-style organised crime which had been implicated in a similar fire which reduced the Teatro Petruzzelli in Bari to a mound of ashes in 1991. Millions of dollars have been received in donations, and after much time-consuming discussions to thrash out whether or not the theatre should be rebuilt as it was, it has been decided to rebuild as before, work hopefully complete in 2002.

One of the world's best loved opera houses, and especially by performers, La Fenice was built in 1792 to replace the San Benedetto, the most beautiful of Venice's seven theatres which burned down in 1774; at first, San Benedetto's owners rebuilt that theatre, only to have to sell it due to an ensuing land dispute. Stripped of their theatre, the owners chose another site, and within just twenty-two months had cleared it of buildings and constructed the very aptly named La Fenice – literally 'the phoenix', the mythical bird that rises again from the ashes. The theatre, with tiers of boxes and costly decorations like La Scala's, was opened with a performance of Giovanni Paisiello's *I giuochi d'Agrigento*, followed by a ballet.

The theatre quickly began to distinguish itself as one of the most important venues in Italy and Europe, and one that significantly helped to shape the history of opera. On 6 February 1813, Gioachino Rossini made his début at La Fenice with *Tancredi*, the first of three operas commissioned for the theatre. Of Vincenzo Bellini's ten operas, two were written for La Fenice – *I Capuleti e I Montecchi* (1830) and *Beatrice di Tenda* (1833).

Gaetano Donizetti, who made his début at La Fenice in 1830 with his opera *Anna Bolena*, considered his second greatest work after *Lucia di Lammermoor*, wrote two other works for the theatre: *Belisario* (1836) and *Maria di Rudenz* (1838). In between these productions, a devastating fire caused the theatre to close in 1837, to be swiftly rebuilt. In 1842, Giuseppe Verdi arrived with *Nabucco*. Two years later he was commissioned to write the first (*Ernani*) of five operas for La Fenice. They were followed by *Attila* (1846), *Rigoletto* (1851), *La traviata* (1853), and *Simon Boccanegra* (1857).

La Fenice was further refurbished inside a number of times after the 1837 fire. There were major repairs at the end of World War I, and again in 1939. In the end, there was really very little if anything left of the original La Fenice. But it gave the desired effect. From the entrance, which was all light, and marble and gilt décor, the impact when looking through into the auditorium, with its Murano chandeliers, and the boxes painted in white and decorated with gold, was both staggering and dreamlike.

The architect: Gianantonio Selva
The building: Opened 1792; fires 1837 and 1996; restoration in progress
Capacity: About 1500
Opening perfomance: Paisiello's *I giuochi d'Agrigento*

Dame Joan Sutherland

Of course, I have beautiful memories of La Fenice, since that is where I made my wonderfully successful début in Handel's *Alcina*, in a production directed by Franco Zeffirelli, and where I was first given the name 'La Stupenda'. It is something that has stuck ever since. I'll be called 'La Stupenda' for the rest of my life.

La Fenice was a gem of theatre, and I was absolutely devastated when it burnt down. It had fantastic acoustics. It came as a terrific shock to hear what had happened, especially since the fire occurred only two years after the Liceu theatre burned down in Barcelona.

The acoustics at the La Fenice were very warm, and yet somehow brilliant at the same time. I fear they will never be able to quite replace it, the way it really was. These old theatres had such wonderful acoustics, often because there was so much wood in them, but that in turn makes them a terrible fire risk.

I have always imagined La Fenice as being a kind of gem, like a piece of jewellery. With all its chandeliers, it used to positively glitter, and of course, in my day, many of the ladies in the audience wore real jewellery. Times haven't changed just a little in that respect, but a lot.

I loved La Fenice. That theatre meant a great deal to me, and not just as an opera house. I mourn it, really.

Massimo De Bernart

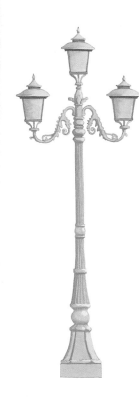

There are three great scandals in Italy: La Fenice in Venice, which has burnt down; the Teatro Petruzzelli of Bari, which burnt down in 1991; and the Teatro Massimo of Palermo, which has been shut for twenty-two years. I fear we will never see any of them again. I am very, very pessimistic. I had strong ties with all these theatres.

La Fenice was warm, it was cosy, and it made you feel safe and snug, as though you were in a little magical room. It was like being inside an 18th century salon – or even, yes, inside a *bonbonnière*. The acoustics were good, it is true, but they were not in my view as incredible as people now say. They were good, that is all. But for me, what was truly wonderful about that theatre was the relationship between the stalls and the orchestra pit. It was absolutely harmonious, and could have been designed by Palladio.

It's difficult to imagine that La Fenice will ever be able to be the same as it was before. In Venice, where I lived for eight years, it's never easy to build anything. It isn't a normal city. And then, La Fenice was false, a wonderful sham, and in the best operatic tradition. And we all knew it. It was pretending – even with decorations that were done relatively recently but, yes, when there were still great craftsmen – to be 18th century. How can that be recreated? And ever since La Fenice burnt down, all that people ever seem to do is to talk . . .

VIENNA
VOLKSOPER

Founded in 1898 by the playwright Adam Müller-Gutenbrunn, the Volksoper was built in an unfashionable part of town with productions of German-language plays and boulevard comedies, often in regional dialects. After a financially troubled start, in 1903 a new administration leased the theatre as a people's opera.

The exterior has an unusual provincial quality, not unlike the repertoire the theatre initially maintained. An unassuming entrance is shielded with a balcony supported by two columns. Turrets with modified onion domes rise in each corner and the whole composition gives the impression of a rural Austrian castle.

After the bombing of the Staatsoper in 1945, the Volksoper served as the main venue for opera for the next ten years. Today the interaction between the two companies is complementary and similar to that between the Paris Opéra and the Opéra Comique.

Nigel Douglas

The Volksoper is exactly what its name suggests, an opera house for the people. Opened in 1898 to celebrate the fiftieth anniversary of Emperor Franz-Joseph's accession to the throne, it never aimed to compete either with the architectural flamboyance or the social éclat of the Court Opera (now the Staatsoper); though once or twice, notably with the introduction to Vienna of *Tosca* (1907) and *Salome* (1910), both of which had been declared by the censors to be too shocking for Imperial eyes and ears, it stole a notable march on its more elevated rival.

It has always been the Volksoper's policy to keep ticket prices low and to perform everything in German, a fact which makes some of its repertoire – the French and Italian operas, for instance – of limited interest to the foreign visitor. The first production I saw there, when I went to live in Vienna as a music student in 1956, was Cole Porter's *Küss mich Kätchen*, which proved such a success that it was followed by Irving Berlin's masterpiece *Annie nimm dein Schiessgewehr*. It is, however, in its capacity as the headquarters of Viennese operetta that the Volksoper establishes its *raison d'être*. Where other opera houses throughout the world are happy to give reasonably regular airings to *Die Fledermaus* or *Die lustige Witwe*, the Volksoper reminds us how many musical treasures are to be encountered in the works of Millöcker, Suppé, Zeller, Ziehrer, Kálmán et al.

Operetta can be the greatest of fun for the performers as well as for the audience, but please let no one make the mistake of assuming that for that reason it must be easy. On the contrary, apart from the sheer vocal magnificence which many grand operas require, operetta is in many ways the more demanding of the two, and never more so than when you find yourself

The architect: Graf & Krauss
The building: Opened 1898
Capacity: About 1470
Opening performance: Weber's *Der Freischutz*
World première: Schönberg's *Die Glückliche Hand*, 1924

in that familiar position of stepping into a production with minimal rehearsal. In opera, as long as you are musically rock solid in your role, nothing much can go wrong – you may exit left when the production requires you to exit right but as long as you do so with conviction who is going to notice?

In operetta, however, you have to cope with dance numbers, and the tenor who starts with his left foot while everyone else starts with their right will be spotted by one and all. It can happen, too, even in the best organised houses (of which the Volksoper is one) that your regular partner has been taken ill, her replacement is someone whom you meet for the first time in your life at the beginning of your Act I dialogue scene, and it rapidly becomes apparent that the text she is using is a version with which you are not familiar. When I made my début at the Volksoper as Danilo in *Die lustige Witwe* in 1964 I was lucky enough to have a soprano partner who was willing to rehearse with me beforehand, but I was introduced to the rest of the cast, the orchestra, the conductor and the stage in the white heat of action.

I was recently engaged to accompany a group of the Friends of Covent Garden to Vienna, and to lecture on the two pieces which they would be attending. One was *Tosca* in the Staatsoper and the other was Emmerich Kálmán's *Die Csárdásfürstin* at the Volksoper. I was left in no doubt as to which the group had enjoyed the more – the Volksoper won hands down.

VIENNA
STAATSOPER

When an expanding Vienna of the 1850s decided to create its now famous Ringstrasse by replacing the ancient walls of the city with a wide boulevard, one of the most prominent sites realised in the scheme was reserved by Emperor Franz Joseph I for a new opera house. An open competition held in 1860 awarded the commission jointly to August Siccard von Siccardsburg for the building and Eduard van der Nüll for the interior. During the entire eight years of construction the project was besieged by scandals of money, design and critics (usually those unsuccessful in the competition) who labelled it 'the Waterloo of architecture'. Originally called the Kaiserlich-Königliches Hofoperntheater, or Hofoper for short (the name was changed to Staatsoper in 1918), the building opened with *Don Giovanni* on 25 May 1869.

Problems continued after the opening. The first director, Franz von Dingelstedt, operated with the philosophy 'concerts are superfluous, opera at best a necessary evil!' In the 1880s the Viennese were treated to the world premières of Goldmark's *Merlin* (1886) and Massenet's *Werther* (1892). Gustav Mahler reigned at the Hofoper for a decade beginning in 1897 with his production of Wagner's *Lohengrin*. His string of successes included Wagner's *Tristan und Isolde* (1903), Beethoven's *Fidelio* (1904) and (radically) faithful productions of the five great Mozart operas. A bust of the later-revered Mahler in the vestibule of the Staatsoper was one of the first objects removed by the Nazis.

Today the opera house stands in essentially its original form. Damaged by Allied bombs in 1945, the Italian Renaissance exterior was salvaged while the auditorium itself had to be completely rebuilt. The new interior is in a modern classical style, not unlike the original but simpler. Structural innovations allowed for loges to be built without obstructions and the opera house now has an audience capacity of 2,200.

The architect: August Siccard von Siccardsburg
The building: Opened 1869; bomb damage 1945, reinaugurated 1955
Capacity: About 2200
Opening perfomance: Mozart's *Don Giovanni*

Zurich
Opernhaus

The pretty little park by the Zurichsee in front of the Opernhaus is a proper setting for this very striking building. The simple new glass porch does not distract attention from the 19th century façade and the new steps leading up to a terrace café bring people closer to the opera house than is the case in many cities where those buildings usually stand in splendid isolation.

In 1849 when Wagner arrived in Zurich as an exile from the Dresden authorities, opera had just started to be performed at the Aktientheater. It was in this theatre that Wagner conducted his own version of *Don Giovanni*. A love affair with a benefactor's wife – Mathilde Wesendonck – was the inspiration for *Tristan und Isolde*.

The present theatre was built to the design of the Viennese architects Fellner and Helmer and opened in 1891. The first international festival of opera was held in 1909 and the first authorised performance of *Parsifal* outside Bayreuth in 1913.

Early on the opera house established an innovative repertoire and attracted a high calibre of international talent. The theatre also encouraged Swiss composers.

Hans Zimmermann ran the theatre from 1937 to 1956 with great success, employing first-rate singers and conductors, and maintaining the resident Tonhalle Orchestra with its fine reputation. The first production of Berg's *Lulu* in 1937 was followed by Paul Hindemith's *Mathis der Maler* in 1938 and *Jeanne d'Arc au bûcher* by Arthur Honegger. The first staged production of Schoenberg's *Moses und Aron* was conducted by Hans Rosbaud, newly appointed to the Tonhalle in 1957.

The directorship of Claus Helmut Drese from 1975 to 1986 was marked by the cycle of

Monteverdi operas conducted by Nikolaus Harnoncourt who introduced period musical instruments to achieve an authentic sound. During Drese's reign the company moved to other premises while the Opernhaus was renovated, reopening in 1984 with Wagner's *Die Meistersinger*. From 1986 Christoph Groszer as artistic director continued to attract well known conductors, producers and singers. He was succeeded in 1991 by Alexander Pereira, who has made the Zurich Opera into one of Europe's liveliest companies.

The architect: Fellner & Hellner
The building: Opened 1891
Capacity: About 1100
Opening perfomance: Wagner's *Lohengrin*

Dr. Beat Unternährer

Zurich Opera House, standing close to the lakeshore, is a Neo-Classical edifice with cupola, an embellishment of the city skyline, visible from a distance when crossing the quays. It opened on 1 October 1891 with a production of *Lohengrin*.

In the 1960s, the prevailing mood was to scorn *fin de siècle* elegance in favour of the sort of bold modernistic statement to be found in Sydney or Chicago. The idea was floated of building an opera house that extended out on to the lake. However, plans were dropped in 1971: too much concrete, too much uninspired, functional architecture and, most important of all, too much money. The old opera house was listed as an historic building and placed under legal protection; the dream of building a new opera house in the city died. The old theatre was restored and modernised, greatly increasing the space available by integrating another structure on the side nearer the lake.

Zurich is renowned for its innovative repertoire. Though not devoted to minority interests or controversal innovation, it is equally no run-of-the-mill theatre with a bland, could-be-anywhere programme. Zurich as a city of opera wants to be known in its own right – not for mimicking Frankfurt, Vienna, Brussels or Milan.

The Opernhaus is basically a repertory theatre, staging about three hundred performances a year. From time to time, it abandons the ensemble in favour of a *semistagione* principle – a series of performances staged with the same company. Many famous singers have been happy to sign up for a season in Zurich; some have even become resident. The quality of stage design and musical direction can compare with any of the world's great opera houses even though the auditorium is quite small and intimate

(1,100 seats). The conductors Ferdinand Leitner, Nello Santi, Nikolaus Harnoncourt and Ralf Weikert take a large measure of the credit for this success. The Monteverdi performances under Harnoncourt/Ponnelle made operatic history. Similarly, the great Mozart cycle – a total of eight works staged by Ponnelle before his untimely death – wrote a chapter in European opera history.

World stars, including Plácido Domingo, José Carreras, Neil Shicoff, Simon Estes, Nicolai Ghiaurov and Mirella Freni, are popular guest performers several times a year. They have helped set the high standards of the Zurich Opera House and become audience favourites.

The combination of international singing stars and some of the most challenging and imaginative musical and stage direction to be found anywhere today is at the core of the theatre's artistic policy, while the many new productions capture opera-goers' imagination. With general interest in new productions much greater than for traditional pieces, the opera house inevitably receives more media attention and the public is prepared to pay more for new productions. As a result, artistic standards are rising all the time.

BIBLIOGRAPHY

Bergan, Ronald, *The Great Theatres of London*, London, 1987

Jarman, Richard, *The London Coliseum: The Story of London's Largest Theatre,* 1981

Mackintosh, Iain and Sells, Michael (eds.), *Curtains!!!,* London, 1982

May, Robin, *A Companion to the Opera*, London, 1977

New Grove Dictionary of Opera, Stanley Sadie (ed.), London, 1992

Opera Now, published monthly, London, various issues/articles 1989-1996

Osborne, Charles, *The Opera House Album*, London, 1979

Piroska, Czelenyi, *AZ Operaház*, Budapest, 1981

Pokrovsky, Boris and Grigorovich, Yuri, *The Bolshoi, Opera and Ballet at the Greatest Theatre in Russia*, New York, 1979

Saint-Petersbourg. Vu par ses architectes, Paris, 1993

Sterneck, Margaret, *Insight Compact Guides: Salzburg,* Apa Publications (HK) Ltd., 1995

Stockdale, F.M. and Deyer, M.R., *The Opera Guide*, London, 1990

Turnbull, Robert, *The Opera Gazetteer*, London, 1988

Vermeil, Jean, *Opéras d'Europe*, Paris, 1990

Vishnevskaya, Galina, *Galina: A Russian Story*, New York, 1984

Zietz, Karyl Lynn, *Opera! The Guide to Western Europe's Great Houses,* Santa Fe, 1991

Andras Kaldor, seen here in his gallery in Dartmouth, surrounded by some of his architectural paintings. In bringing together the arts of painting and architecture he has portrayed many other world-famous buildings.

His book *New York – Masterpieces of Architecture* illustrates the gracious buildings of the late 19th/early 20th century built by the city fathers and rich industrialists, and contrasts these with the glass and steel structures of the later 20th century.

In the same series, *Berlin – Masterpieces of Architecture*, Kaldor's architectural paintings depict forty buildings, old and new, many illustrating the remarkable regeneration of the city.

Andras Kaldor, 15 Newcomen Road, Dartmouth, Devon TQ6 9BN
Telephone 01803 833874 Fax: 01803 835161
Email: andras@kaldor.com Website: www.kaldor.com

ANTIQUE COLLECTORS' CLUB
Sandy Lane, Old Martlesham, Woodbridge, Suffolk IP12 4SD, UK
Tel: 01394 389950 Fax: 01394 389999
Email: sales@antique-acc.com Website: www.antique-acc.com
———————— *or* ————————
Market Street Industrial Park, Wappinger's Falls, NY 12590, USA
Tel: 845 297 0003 Fax: 845 297 0068
Email: info@antiquecc.com Website: www.antiquecc.com